MW01490459

How to Speed Read People:

Think Like a Psychologist, Analyze Human Behavior, and Decode Emotions

By Patrick King
Social Interaction and
Conversation Coach at
www.PatrickKingConsulting.com

Table of Contents

Chapter 1. People Analysis

And how does that make you feel?

That's our typical conception of what a psychologist does. They'll ask questions, they'll invite you to talk about yourself, and then they'll sit back and reply with even more follow-up questions.

Indeed, deeply understanding people's histories, experiences, and emotions will certainly let you analyze and read them. Suppose you ask someone about their parents, their upbringing, their past relationships, and how happy they are with their job. You interview them for two hours and ask probing questions, ranging from interview to interrogation style. Armed with just a little bit of insight and psychology, you can now make a pretty reasonable hypothesis as to how they handle issues or how their worldview might be slanted to a certain view.

In other words, this kind of deliberate interaction with someone can help you understand them better.

But none of this really helps you reach the goal of analyzing and understanding people *in a flash, from first glance, or purely from observation.* That is an entirely different skillset, and poses an entirely different set of challenges to overcome.

In this book, I want to help you *think* like a psychologist without necessarily *being* one–i.e., I want to show you how to analyze people quickly, and without loads and loads of data.

Why would you want to learn how to analyze people quickly? There are a variety of reasons.

We want to understand them before they open their mouths. We want to be able to see their motivations. We want to be able to protect ourselves. We want to be able to connect and communicate better. We want to be more emotionally intelligent. We want to categorize people so we can treat them more appropriately. We want to know how to appeal to them, romantically or not. We want to be able to tell if they are lying or what their true emotions are, despite their words to the contrary.

You probably have your own reasons for wanting to master this skill, and for picking up this book.

Yet one of the bigger benefits is that through knowing what to look for in others, we can actually better understand ourselves. Lacking an understanding of yourself means that you won't know why you're behaving in certain ways. You may not understand how or why you got to where you currently are. More importantly, you won't be able to decipher your own needs and wants in situations. You are more or less winging it on a daily basis if you don't apply some of these same principles to yourself.

Take a simple day-to-day activity of exercise to illustrate the importance of having greater self-awareness. If a man knows that he is more of an introvert, he may opt to invest his time in solitary activities and choose to use headphones at the gym to keep to himself. He would likely spend a lot of time avoiding people, and he'd be well aware of that. He would use his exercise sessions as an opportunity to recharge from the outside world and gather himself. If he was an extrovert, he might rather take a cycling class or work out with a few friends at the local park. He would likely seek to add a social element to most of his daily activities, because that's what makes him feel good and energized.

Introvert or extrovert, both people in the example above know how to place themselves in situations they know are best for them, otherwise they might engage in self-sabotage on a daily basis. Had the introvert not known what pushed him over the edge, he could have had an anxiety attack when walking into a high-energy aerobics class. Or, had the extrovert embarked on a five-hour solo hiking excursion to the woods, he might have been bored out of his mind.

Knowing yourself and possessing self-awareness allows you to make more mindful decisions that are right for you. The more that you are well-acquainted with yourself, the more you'll also see that your identity and purpose are wholly within your control. If that's a side benefit to understanding how to analyze people better, it's a pretty powerful one.

Our understanding of others needs to grow in tandem with our understanding of ourselves. That's why you might find that as you read through the chapters that follow, you flip back and forth between your own perspective and those of other people. Remember that you cannot fully recognize and understand a trait in someone else if you lack the self-awareness to consider that trait's expression in yourself.

It was the inimitable Albert Einstein that once said, "If I had an hour to solve a problem I'd spend 55 minutes thinking about the problem and five minutes thinking about solutions." Just like the pithy example with the man and his choice of exercise, when we can understand the parameters that we are working in (and that other people are also working in), including but not limited to values, perspectives, self-identity, and overall personality, everything else can flow more smoothly.

Analyzing people is certainly a skill that has wide applicability—but it's not necessarily from asking probing questions like a psychologist or observing people's body language and cues like an FBI interrogator, even though we will go into depth about those kinds of methods later on.

There are multiple angles that contribute to a holistic view of a person, and it's only through taking them all together that we can be accurate. For this reason, it's helpful to start from the beginning in terms of how people used to think about identity and personality in the past. This historical grounding will give you a general overview not just of one or two chosen psychological models, but of all models, and the broader function they can serve. It's about learning *how* to think about people's behaviors and the motivations behind them.

For instance, when you seek to read and analyze someone, should you be looking at their inherent temperament or rather to their environment? Are they learned or innately part of one's destiny? Are we slaves to our genetics and destined to be like our parents? Can we find an answer to what has been an ongoing debate and the subject of study by psychologists, scientists, and philosophers for decades? We'll get there.

A Brief History of Analyzing

To understand how we arrived at the modern take on personality and identity that can inform our analyzing, it's helpful to start from a historical perspective. As long as there have been people, there have been people trying to understand people! There have been countless myths and models all throughout history that have attempted to explain the mysteries of human personality. It comes as no surprise that one of the earliest *formal* theories stems from philosophers in ancient Greece. The Greeks first theorized that one could classify types of personalities and temperaments through "humors." This was called *humorism*.

It was Hippocrates (460–370 BC), considered one of the founding fathers of Western medicine, who first developed and defined humorism as a medical theory. He believed that a person's mood and emotions came from an excess of four specific bodily fluids: yellow bile, black bile, blood, and phlegm. Thus, in varying amounts, these represented a person's personality traits and general temperaments. As a follow-up, in Galen's (129–c.200 AD) dissertation *De Temperamentis*, he studied and developed the typology of these temperaments. He was determined to find the physiological reasons behind people's behaviors.

Derived from the four elements of air, earth, wind, and fire, Galen classified these behaviors as being either hot or cold and dry or wet components. A balance between the qualities was also something that could be possible and what Galen worked to prove as being the ideal personality. Galen theorized that an ideal personality comprised a complementary balance of hot or cold and dry or wet.

However, eventually realizing that such balance was unlikely to characterize most people in society, he eventually codified four primary temperaments: choleric, melancholic, sanguine, and phlegmatic. These were respectively named after the bodily humors that Hippocrates noted. When humors would excessively produce, this would create an imbalance in paired qualities.

What's important about humorism is not necessarily whether it's true or not, but rather the *kind* of model it is, and how it works to explain and predict human behavior. In fact, any time you take a modern personality test (or even a quick quiz in a fashion magazine!) you are utilizing the intellectual roots of Galen.

The idea is that human beings exist in a limited number of *types or categories*, and that these psychological types are biologically grounded. This may seem pretty obvious to modern sensibilities, but that's only because we're now so familiar with the concept. Galen's theory encompassed more than just human personality; rather, the human being as a whole was embedded in a rich symbolic world of interconnected parts of a whole Total wellbeing was a matter of harmony and balance between heaven and earth, body and soul, or even (from the Eastern point of view) yin and yang.

Here are the four main humors and their corresponding temperamental types–see if you can recognize some themes and patterns that persist even to today:

Yellow Bile: Choleric Temperament. This person is characterized as being confident, ambitious, overbearing, and passionate. This strong-willed personality tends to be more extroverted than introverted.

This humor corresponds to summer, the gallbladder, and the elements of hotness and dryness. These manifest in the body as ambition, drive, and leadership. The negative aspect of having choleric temperament is anger or domination of others, but the positive side is a person with charisma and energy. As you can imagine, this type was associated with great military or political figures.

Black Bile: Melancholic Temperament. Melancholics tend to be reserved and thoughtful. They can be moody and expect a high level of perfectionism. They also value alone time and are mindful of making decisions.

This humor corresponds to the dryness and coldness of autumn. Those with a melancholic temperament can be creative, artistic, kind, and insightful, but may also be depressive and likely to despair all of life's tragedies.

Blood: Sanguine Temperament. No social event can be without the social butterflies–quite literally, they are the "lifeblood" and "heart" of the party! Sanguine temperaments are people-oriented and are deemed to be the "happy-go-lucky" types.

This humor is associated with the newness and exuberance of spring, with the vitality of the liver, the element of air, with wetness and hotness, and with the life-giving properties of the blood. Sanguine temperaments are cheerful and lively, but their energy can be scattered and disorganized, with its worst expression being a kind of mania.

Phlegm: Phlegmatic Temperament. Loyalty and consistency are the best terms to describe phlegmatic types. They are quiet and stable, traits that other people appreciate for keeping their relationships more balanced. They can also be seen as submissive due to their overly trustworthy behaviors.

Corresponding to winter (wet and cold) this type is associated with the lungs and the element of water. Phlegmatics can be dependable administrators and diplomats, but their constancy can sometimes turn to laziness or resistance to change.

Many people will identify with some, if not all, of these humors. That's to be expected, since Galen believed that each of us is composed of some unique blend of each of these temperamental "ingredients." There may be particular days or situations that cause people to portray one or more of these temperaments at any given time; for example, springtime can make everyone feel more sanguine, and wet and cold foods were believed to promote the phlegmatic humor, and dampen down the hotness and dryness of an overly choleric temperament. Generally speaking, however, one type of humor will be more dominant over the others on a consistent basis.

Overall, *humorism* greatly centers around the individual possessing unique compositions, like a standard recipe with deviations here and there to add some personality and flavor.

However, humorism never explained the *reasons* behind an individual's personality. Different humors may have aggregated in different amounts in people, but why? What caused certain humoral imbalances in the first place? Was it just a birthright? A curse? The will of the gods? Still, in practice the theory worked similarly to what we are learning to do with this book. With humorism, you would observe someone and then categorize their composition of humors; in the same way, we are trying to glean information about people through observations and then make conclusions about their *most consistent* character, overall tendencies, and traits. Humors may not be so helpful in the modern age, but the theory demonstrates humankind's long-standing interest in understanding self-identity and categorizing other people into knowable types.

Fast-forward a few hundred years and famous Austrian psychologist Sigmund Freud (1856–1939) came up with his own way of describing someone's personality and identity. Perhaps the best-known model of personality, though somewhat dubious in real-life effectiveness and application, is known as the *structural model of personality*. You know it as the three components of the *id, ego, and superego*.

Freud believed that a person's psyche was centrally controlled by these three unconscious components, which were locked in eternal battle. He also believed that each component had a direct influence over the other, thus shaping someone's personality. Just like humorism, if there was any imbalance between the three components, it would give rise to certain types of personalities and identities (and related disorders).

We won't delve into too much detail here (and there is much detail to be delved into!), but what follows is a very brief summary of the "topographical" features of the human psyche according to Freud.

Id: "Just give it to me; I want it now." The id follows the pleasure principle. Basically, a person will behave solely in a manner to collect a reward in the end. The id is the primitive and instinctive component of all three. As such, it functions solely on fulfilling those primal drives, such as hunger, sex, and all forms of pleasure. It is a single-minded drive.

An infant is the perfect representation of the id because an infant only knows what it wants and cries when it is not received. Infants are impulsive and lack the ability to empathize or control themselves. It's only later that a newborn can actually develop an ego and superego through learned situations. The infant wanting dessert has no regard for reality. Instead, he is wishful in his thinking and wants that dessert if it's the last thing he'll ever get. This is where ego comes into play.

Ego: "I really want that, but how can I realistically get it?" The id can't last forever in the real world in conjunction with other people and their own needs.

The ego eventually takes over the id as the principle of reality. It helps a person acknowledge that there are limitations and external factors to someone's behavior. The same child will learn that he may not always get a dessert, especially if he acts up and throws his food around the kitchen. These were factors that weren't ever-present before and he's able to acknowledge now.

Think of the ego as being the mediator between the struggles of unrealistic id and reality. Basically, this is where a child learns to make decisions while actually weighing consequences and things other than bare desire. Reasoning is one characteristic of the ego as opposed to the more irrational id. The ego works by strategizing realistic ways to meet the demands of the id.

This process usually means that there must be a compromise at some point. Sometimes, it's necessary to postpone rewards so that one won't feel the negative consequences when reacting irrationally. The ego is more aware of social norms and decencies, thus teaching a person how to compose himself/herself in situations. There's no right or wrong. The goal of the ego is to attain reward without harm. In a power struggle, the ego will always fall to the id. But then there's the superego.

Superego: "I want that, but not if it makes me a terrible person." The superego helps the individual identify values and morals set by society and forces him or her to be more self-aware. Basically, the superego is the conscience sitting on your shoulder and asking whether you should do something or not.

The superego can also be seen to suppress the primal urges of the id, but in a different way from the ego. Remember, the ego suppresses the id by reminding it of the practical realities of the world, while the superego suppresses the id by giving a test of values and morals before acting.

And how do these three elements manifest? Suppose an infant initially believed that he could finish his meal and then a dessert would always come after (his id). However, he didn't account for other factors while he ate his dinner. If he threw his food around and made a mess, he learned that this was deemed as a negative behavior that could alter his happy ending (his ego). Finally, he felt shameful about disrespecting his parents and learned to correct his behavior in the future (his superego).

Overall, Freud concluded that the three components of the psyche all had their own interests at play. This is what caused a person to think and act in a particular way. The child first acted out of selfishness and eventually learned to channel his emotions not only in favor of himself, but also to meet social norms.

Many psychologists were greatly influenced by the works and studies of Freud. But the fact that his structural theory relies completely on unconscious drives makes it nearly impossible to prove and quantify. It becomes too inconsistent without data to study and confirm the id's or ego's existence and role. Thus, it can necessarily only remain a theory, which isn't so helpful for our goals of analyzing people from objective data points and psychological phenomena. Yet again, it is part of the puzzle of analyzing people because it shows the different forces that can drive people's behavior.

If we're looking for more hard data and evidence on how to analyze others, we will need to start looking at anthropology and biology. That's exactly what started to happen once the technology was sufficiently advanced. One biological perspective of identity is that the range of personalities and traits we display are a result of natural selection. In other words, the traits that people have now were more vital to their ancestors, and what remains are only the most useful of traits. The well-known principle of "survival of the fittest" is considered to have created at least the baseline for our modern personalities.

Over time, survival of the fittest made people begin to develop characteristics that are split into two specific categories: *intrasexual* traits and *intersexual* traits. These are the two types of traits that assist in proliferating as a species.

Intrasexual traits are what attract the opposite sex. They are mating displays, how we instinctually emphasize masculinity or femininity, charm and wit, and generally what feelings of love and affection are drawn from. When two people meet, they display particular traits that keep the other interested and engaged. The better they are at these traits, the more successful they are with mating and dating. Over time, these became instinctual behaviors that inform our personalities.

Intersexual traits are what allow us to defeat rivals of the same sex for mating, dating, relationships, and all goals involving the opposite sex. In other words, how we compete and win. These traits ask the question, what makes us a more desirable mate than someone else? They make us more feminine or masculine, but this time in an attempt to stand out. Over time, these competitive drives also became instinctual parts of our identities, and of course, people possess them to various degrees.

In terms of the direct physiological structure of our brains, contemporary scientists found that there is a direct correlation between the sizes of various brain structures and different personality traits. At the University of Minnesota, a study asked subjects to answer a series of questions pertaining to personality.

Then the subjects were also given a brain-imaging test where specific regions of their brains were photographed and studied.

The data set consisted of categorizing the study participants into five different factors for personality traits, the Big Five, which will be covered in greater detail shortly:

- conscientiousness
- agreeableness
- extraversion
- openness to experience
- neuroticism

The following conclusions were found:

- Researchers were able to discover that extroverted people tend to have a bigger medial orbitofrontal cortex. This is located right above and behind the eyes.
- People considered to be more conscientious had larger lateral prefrontal cortexes.
- Neurotically driven individuals had bigger brain regions such as the cortices, which meant this was responsible for their negative emotions.
- Agreeable people also had larger cortical regions. However, as opposed to neurotic people, these regions are a little more wrinkled and folded. This means they are

able to empathize with others and their thoughts.

- It is still unclear as to how brain regions correspond with openness and intellect.

The results speak for themselves. They could now directly relate a person's brain graph to how this person behaves. There is a very real biological basis for differences in personality and identity. Nature versus nurture is always a compelling debate, and this demonstrates that they will always be inseparable.

While it's not quite practical to subject friends new and old to a brain imaging scan to understand their personality better, we're starting to get closer to the focus of this book: being able to read and analyze people through observations and objective data points.

Takeaways:

- Seeking to analyze people and discover personality and identity has been a compelling issue for as long as we have been sentient beings. To understand ourselves is to make the best decisions, and to understand others provides the ability to make the most out of interactions, whatever your goal. Like many disciplines, study seems to have begun in ancient Greece with the theory of humorism—where four separate bodily fluids were present in the body in varying quantities that gave rise to different personalities and four temperaments in particular.

- One of the most seminal personality theories was put forth by Sigmund Freud hundreds of years later. This is known as the structural model, and you know it by its three components: the id, ego, and superego. Like the humors, they worked together in varying amounts to form a unique personality. The id is a hedonist, the ego is the mediator, while the superego is the conscience.

- There is also a strong biological basis for differences in personality, identity, and the traits we might analyze in others. First, intrasexual and intersexual traits have formed the baseline for our modern personalities in many ways. Second, there are literal biological and physical differences between those who score differently on the Big Five personality traits.

- Why does this all matter? Well, there are far too many reasons we might want to understand the people around us better and more quickly. And if you don't know where you yourself are coming from and where you are right now, how are you supposed to know where you should go next?

Chapter 2. Test Your Personality

Now, any discussion of analyzing personality and identity would be incomplete without delving into the Big Five personality traits, as well as the Meyers-Briggs Type Indicator (MBTI) and associated Keirsey Temperaments. These are direct ways of understanding who someone is, to the extent that such tests can be accurate. In fact, you've probably already encountered the MBTI in your own life, or have at least a passing familiarity with its terminology.

Today, full MBTI type tests take time to complete and need to be scored and interpreted by a professional psychometrist. Very rarely will you possess this amount of knowledge about someone you want to read or analyze, but again, it's worth understanding a few different scales upon which to evaluate others. You might be able to identify some of these traits in others and then understand their motivations and values as a result.

Chances are, at some point in your life, you've taken a personality, career aptitude, or relationship test to learn more about yourself. In the context of analyzing people, this isn't quite going to get us where we want. Using these personality tests almost defeats the purpose of analyzing someone based on observations and behaviors, but they do provide plenty of food for thought in exactly what traits to look for and what differentiates people. Such theoretical frameworks give us what can be thought of as a broad sketch or outline–it is our own, spontaneous, everyday observations that will help us fill in the rest of the picture.

Hopefully, you've stumbled across one that sought to evaluate you based on the Big Five personality traits. As previously mentioned, this is a theory that breaks down the human psyche into five broad characteristics. These five simple factors could determine the very complex question you've been chasing: what makes you *you*—and what makes other people *them*?

The Big Five

It's a theory that dates back to 1949, in research published by D.W. Fiske. Since then, it's been gaining popularity and has been written about by the likes of Norman (1967),

Smith (1967), Goldberg (1981), and McCrae and Costa (1987). Instead of evaluating you as a whole based on your experiences and motivations, this theory reduces you down to five traits: openness to experience, conscientiousness, extroversion, agreeableness, and neuroticism. We can see echoes of Galen's theory here–can you spot the overlap between the following types and the four humors?

You may have heard of the Big 5 terms before. Terms like introvert and extrovert are thrown around a lot these days, but what do they really mean? They're two ends of the spectrum. Each trait has two extremes, and although we may not want to admit it, every one of us embodies all of these five traits to some degree. According to this theory, it's how much of each and where we land in the range between the extremes that determine our unique personality.

Openness to Experience. The first of the Big Five personality traits determines how willing you are to take risks or try something new. Would you ever jump out of a plane? How about pack up and move halfway around the world to immerse yourself in a new culture? If your answer to both of those questions was a resounding yes, then you probably score high in your openness to experience. You seek out the unknown.

At one extreme, people who are high in openness are curious and imaginative. They go in search of new adventures and experiences. They seem to want to learn new things simply for the sake of it. They can get bored easily and turn to their creativity to uncover new interests and even daring activities. These people are flexible and seek out variety in their daily life. For them, routine is not an option. At the other end of the spectrum, people who are low on the openness scale prefer continuity and stability to change. They are practical, sensible, and more conventional than their peers. Change is not their friend.

In the real world, most people fall somewhere between these opposites, but where you find yourself on the spectrum could reveal a lot about who you are and what you excel at.

Do you dream of being a CEO or at the head of your field, for instance? Openness has been linked to leadership. If you're able to entertain new ideas, think outside the box, and adapt quickly to new situations, you're more likely to become and succeed as a leader (Lebowitz, 2016). One way to think of openness to experience is to consider someone's reaction and attitude towards the unknown. Are they instantly put on edge, or does the unknown actually seem a little exciting?

It was Apple cofounder Steve Jobs's decision to audit a calligraphy class in 1973 that would lead to the groundbreaking typography in Mac computers years later. At the time, no one associated computers with beautiful fonts, but Jobs saw something that no one else could. He embraced the calligraphy class, sought to change the way people thought about computers, and opened himself up to a new vision of the future.

Conscientiousness. This is the personality trait that makes you careful and cautious. You're vigilant in your actions and often think twice, or three times, before making a decision, especially if it wasn't in your original plans. People with this trait have high standards, and intend to keep them. It's all about doing your job and your duty–and doing it well. I'm sure you can think of one or two people in your world who are like this!

Those who have high levels of conscientiousness tend to be extremely focused on their goals. They plan things out, focusing on the detailed tasks at hand, and they stick to their schedules. They have better control over their impulses, emotions, and behaviors, such that they are able to focus more of their energy on their professional success. While they may not live as adventurously as their peers, they do tend to live longer, thanks in part to their healthier habits.

At the other end of the spectrum, people who are not so conscientious tend to be more impulsive and disorganized. They become demotivated by too much structure, can procrastinate on important work, and have a weaker ability to control their behavior. This is the person who suddenly loses interest in a task the moment the task is scheduled and planned out in detail. Overall, there is less control, over both the environment and the self. This can lead to more self-destructive habits, such as smoking and substance abuse, and an overall inability to get things done. Impulse control is no easy feat for them.

So how conscientious are you? Do you like schedules at work but still find yourself avoiding exercise when you get home? You may embrace some aspects of conscientiousness, like schedules and to-do lists, and not others, like exercising or performing other healthy habits. Most people land somewhere in the middle of the conscientiousness spectrum, but if you can find ways to embrace planning and order a little bit more, you could be setting yourself up for success.

Conscientiousness has been linked to better success after training (Woods, Patterson,

Koczwara & Sofat, 2016), more effective job performance (Barrick & Mount, 1991), higher job satisfaction, and careers with greater prestige and higher incomes (Judge, Higgins, Thoresen & Barrick, 1999). A study by Soldz and Vaillant (1999) also found that high levels of conscientiousness have helped people better adjust to the challenges of life that will inevitably sneak up on you.

Conscientiousness is the preventative medicine we could all use to stop problems before they start.

Extroversion. Extroversion is one of those traits that is often misunderstood–especially in the public consciousness. We tend to assume that this is the trait that defines how outgoing or social you are. We think that extroverts are the life of the party, that they've got lots of energy, and that they know how to talk. While this may often be true, it's not actually the defining quality of extroversion. Rather, extroverts are *people who find social situations energizing, rather than draining*. Extroverts draw their energy from being around other people and thrive on being the center of attention. For that reason, they maintain a wide circle of friends and take every opportunity to meet new people.

At the other extreme are people who often find extroverts exhausting to be around: introverts. These are people may be very friendly and may also have lots of friends, but their battery is depleted by social interaction, not charged up. They are charged up by spending time on their own. Introverts aren't necessarily shy; introversion also does not mean social anxiety or poor social skills. Rather, introversion is a preference. These are people who simply prefer solitude to socializing, or calm to chaos.

Do you wish office parties would never end, or do you feel drained after about an hour? Do you enjoy meeting new people, or would you prefer to be cuddled up at home with a good book? Are you a morning person, or do you truly wake up when the sun goes down?

If you're often the last one to leave a social gathering, you enjoy being around people, and you thrive on the late-night hours, you likely rank high on the extroversion scale. If, on the other hand, you dread the thought of going to parties, would rather stay home alone, and prefer to wake up bright and early to start your day, you're probably more of an introvert.

Depending on the day, you may be inclined to go either way. However, by and large, people typically place somewhere along the spectrum between the two.

Agreeableness. This is the trait that identifies how kind and sympathetic you are and how warm and cooperative you are with others. It's the desire to get along with others and the tendency to value social harmony, cohesion, and peace. .

Do you tend to take a big interest in other people and their problems? When you see others going through difficulties, does it affect you, too? If you're empathetic and caring toward others and driven by the desire to help, you may be quite an agreeable person. You feel their pain and are driven to do something about it. Those high in agreeableness are amiable and empathetic. They like finding the middle-ground, and work hard to consider and accommodate others.

At the other end of the spectrum, people who are less agreeable may find they take less of an interest in other people's lives. Instead of trying to work together to solve a problem, they may be more content to go it alone. They're not agreeable because they are determined to do exactly what they want to do–regardless of how that affects other people. Because of their nature, they may often be perceived as offensive or unpleasant to be around. On the other hand, they are seldom influenced by group pressures and can be nonconformists.

We all have different thresholds for how much we're willing to do for others and how much we're willing to work together. That limit is where you rank on the agreeableness spectrum.

Why people are so agreeable is still up for debate. For some, it's the genuine concern for the well-being of others. For others, it's the result of social pressure and accepted norms– there is a strong human desire to belong and be accepted by the "tribe." Fear of consequences can also be a motivating factor. Some agreeable people may be acting that way because they are petrified of social confrontation. Whatever the case, research has shown that agreeable people are rarely cruel, ruthless, or selfish (Roccas, Sagiv, Schwartz & Knafo, 2002). If you're looking for ways to be a little bit happier, figuring out where you lie on the agreeable index may be a good place to start.

Neuroticism. We all have those days when nothing is how it seems. You think your coworkers are out to get you. You're so anxious you can't sleep. You feel like you're caught in a Woody Allen film. But if you find yourself having lots of those days, to the point where you feel more down than you do up, you may have high levels of the last of the Big Five traits: neuroticism. This is the personality trait that essentially measures how emotionally stable you are. It identifies your ability to remain steady and balanced versus anxious, insecure, or constantly distracted.

Neurotics tend to approach life with a high dose of anxiety. They overthink, then they overthink their tendency to overthink. They worry more than most and their moods can shift quickly and with little prompting. This kind of behavior can make them prone to being stressed or even depressed.

Those on the less neurotic side of the spectrum tend to be more emotionally stable. When stress comes their way, they have an easier time dealing with it. Bouts of sadness are few and far between, and they see fewer reasons to stress about whatever may come their way. These are those calm, zen-like people able to be in the moment.

Do you find yourself using humor to cope with a challenge, or do problems tend to stress you out? Are you pretty levelheaded all day long, or do you switch from hot to cold in a heartbeat? If you take things in stride and usually only have one mood per day, you're probably less neurotic than others. But if you have many moods in the space of a short amount of time and are anxious more often than not, you're probably on the more neurotic side.

However, being neurotic doesn't have to be all doom and gloom. After all, worrying about our health is what keeps us taking vitamins and visiting the doctor's office for checkups. In that case, the anxiety of neurotics may actually keep them one step ahead in many ways.

In the end, we have five scales that have been proven to at least be major elements of personality for you to evaluate people on. Some chapters in this book will give you a type of checklist of elements to look for in analyzing them quickly—here, we can make observations, look at where people might fall on the Big Five traits, and then extrapolate outward from there.

Another such scale is the Myers-Briggs Type Indicator (MBTI) as well as the subsequent Keirsey Temperaments.

Jung and the MBTI

The MBTI has been one of the most popular methods for people to evaluate and categorize themselves—of course, this means we should understand it to categorize *others*. Overall, the test is based on four very distinct *dichotomies*, which you can imagine as simply being traits, similar to the Big Five traits. People have compared the MBTI as one that purely functions as a modern horoscope. Of course, no test is foolproof, and this doesn't mean that it still can't provide you with important insight into a person's character or identity.

The MBTI was developed around the time of World War II. Myers and Briggs were two housewives and observed many people taking job opportunities willy-nilly. However, it bothered them that many of those people were taking jobs that didn't necessarily pertain to their skills. They combined their observations with the work of psychologist Carl Jung, who believed that archetypes came from models of people, behavior, and their personalities. He strongly suggested that these archetypes came innately due to the influence of human behavior.

Thus, the MBTI was developed with the intention of helping people find jobs and careers that were better suited to their innate personalities. As mentioned, there are four general dichotomies or traits:

- For personality, the spectrum is extroverted (E) to introverted (I).
- For perception, the spectrum is sensing (S) to intuition (N).
- For judging, the spectrum is thinking (T) to feeling (F).
- For implementation, the spectrum is judging (J) to perceiving (P).

The idea is that everyone can measure themselves along these four spectrums, and certain patterns will emerge so that you are able to discover your personality type.

The first dichotomy, extraversion versus introversion, signifies the source as well as the direction of a person's energy expression. Note that this is defined slightly differently from the Big Five trait of extroversion.

An extrovert and his energy expression mainly happen in the external world. When in the presence and company of others, extroverts are able to recharge. For an introvert, his source of energy mainly happens in his internal world. Having space to himself or herself is ideal and can prove to be the best mode of recharging that energy expression.

Extroverted people are action-oriented in comparison to introverted people, who are more thought-oriented. For instance, in a classroom, extroverted students like to participate in group discussions and presentations. Their interactions with other students provide that sense of charge for their personality types. An introverted student would rather work alone on projects and feel somewhat uncomfortable during whole class discussions. They like being able to think on their own and work through assessments by themselves as well.

The second dichotomy, sensing versus intuition, represents how someone perceives information.

When a person is sensing, he or she believes information received directly from that external world. This may come in the form of using their five senses—sight, smell, touch, taste, and hearing. Decisions come in more immediate and experience-based ways.

For someone using intuition, he or she believes information from an internal world—their intuition—over external evidence. This comes in the form of having that "gut feeling." He or she digs a little deeper into detail and tries to connect patterns. It may take a little longer before a decision can be made.

Sensing has to do with believing information that is more concrete and tangible over intuition, which is more about looking at the underlying theories or principles that may come out of data. A police officer will always use evidence and data to support their claims for making an arrest because this information is measurable. On the other side, a lawyer would exhibit more intuition because there could be a lot more to the context being presented, which helps him defend his clients.

The third dichotomy, thinking versus feeling, has to do with how a person processes information. Thinking is when someone makes a decision mainly through the process of logical thinking. They also think in tangible means, where they look to rules to guide their decision-making.

Opposite to this is the feeling where someone would rather make a decision based on emotion. For decisions, these people look to what they value as a means for choosing their best option. They may deem thinkers as being cold and heartless.

Thinking mostly occurs when someone lays out all the possible and practical reasons for making a sound decision. Basically, someone is going to make a decision using their brain. Feeling is when someone will make that decision from the heart. People who purchase homes will either sign the paperwork based on pricing and resale value (thinking) versus those buying to stay in their old neighborhoods (feeling).

The fourth dichotomy, judging versus perceiving, is how someone will implement the information he has processed.

Organizing life events is how someone would judge and later use it, as a rule, to stick to the plan. These people like to have order and structure. Their sense of self-control comes from being able to control their environments as much as possible. Judging types will normally use previous experiences as a catalyst to either continue or avoid certain behaviors later. They also like to see things settled and done with.

Improvisation and option exploration is what someone would do with perceiving. These people like having options and see organization as being a limit to their potential. They like to make choices when they are necessary and like to explore problem-solving and strategizing. Perceiving types will somewhat live in the moment and understand that there are multitudes of options available to them, regardless of how other experiences have occurred in the past.

There are a total of 16 different combinations, or personality types, which can come out of the permutations of preferences in the mentioned four dichotomies. These help to represent one of the two poles that each person can have in terms of a dominant dichotomy. So this is what defines the 16 different personality types, as each can be assigned a four-letter acronym.

So for instance, ESFJ would stand for extroverted, sensing, feeling, and judging. These people might be those you see on television sitcoms who gossip about everyone and whose main goal in life is to be married with kids, only to be able to gossip with other moms around the neighborhood. Of course, this is a categorization so stereotypical that it hurts, but nonetheless, observing and categorizing someone based on these four simple letters can unlock a deeper understanding of anyone.

A vast shortcoming is that the MBTI only gives answers that are definitive, and it doesn't account for the fact that people are usually not one-sided on their traits. People aren't entirely on one end of the spectrum over another. The MBTI only gives people two ends of the spectrum, not anything in between. Thus, most people can be moderate in many other traits. For instance, you might be 45% extroverted and 55% introverted, but the MBTI would call you an introvert without subtlety.

Another shortcoming rests not with the MBTI itself, but with the fact that we are all changing throughout our lifetimes. Professor David Pittenger of Marshall University found that when a retest of the MBTI is conducted over a short amount of time, as many as 50% of people will get classified into a different type.

Over time and as expected, people can change. Results from their MBTIs can change in a span of either days or weeks depending on their moods or influences from their external and internal environments. These factors will say nothing about their actual personality types.

Keirsey's Temperaments

One popular way of understanding the MBTI is through David Keirsey's four temperaments. He helped to organize the information people received from the MBTI to narrow it down from 16 personality types to four general temperaments instead. Within each temperament Keirsey also identified two types of roles one might play instinctively and naturally.

Temperament One: The Guardian

This happens when someone results in being a sensor and judger. These people have a longing to belong, contribute to their society, and are confident in their own abilities.

Guardians are also concrete and more organized. They seek security and belonging while still being concerned with responsibilities and duties. Logistics is one of their greatest strengths; they are excellent at organization, facilitation, supporting, and checking. Their two roles are administrators and conservators.

Administrators tend to be the proactive and directive versions of guardians. They are most efficient in regulating. Conservators are the reactive and expressive versions of guardians and their best intelligence is supporting.

Temperament Two: The Artisan

This occurs when an individual tests as being a sensor and perceiver. These individuals live freely and through a lot of action-filled events.

Artisans are completely adaptable. They usually seek out stimulation and virtuosity. Artisans are highly concerned with making a large impact, and one of their greatest strengths happens to be tactics. They are extremely proficient in troubleshooting, problem-solving, and agility. They also have the ability to manipulate tools, instruments, and equipment.

Artisans have two roles—operators and entertainers. Operators are the directive and proactive version of artisans. They have a high capacity to expedite and are the attentive crafters and promoters of the role variants. Entertainers are the more informative and reactive versions of artisans. They have a great way of improvising and are attentive to details.

Keirsey estimates that about 80% of the population is categorized as being artisans or guardians.

Temperament Three: The Idealist

This happens when someone results in being an intuitive and feeler. These people find meaning in their lives while helping themselves and others be the best versions of themselves. They value uniqueness and individuality.

Idealists are abstract and can be compassionate. They work to seek significance and meaning in almost everything. They are concerned with their own personal growth and being able to find their true identities. They are very good at diplomacy and have strengths in clarifying, unifying, individualizing, and inspiring others. They have two roles— mentors and advocates.

Mentors are the proactive and directive versions of idealists. They are very good at developing and their attentive variant roles are counselors and teachers. Advocates are the reactive and informative idealists who are very good at mediating.

Temperament Four: The Rational

This occurs when someone tests as being an intuitive and thinker. There is always a drive to increase these people's knowledge, and they are highly competent. They usually have a sense of personal satisfaction.

Rationals are objective and abstract. They seek to be masters of their craft and have self-control. They are usually concerned with their own type of knowledge and competence. Strategy is their greatest strength, and they have the ability to logically investigate, engineer, conceptualize, theorize, and coordinate. Their two roles are coordinators and engineers.

Coordinators are the proactive and directive versions of rationals. They are great at arranging and their variant roles are masterminds and field marshals. Engineers are the reactive and informative versions of rationals.

Keirsey's temperaments have the ability to take personality trait assessment a few steps deeper than that of the MBTI. It helps to evaluate a person's results as they relate to other traits while the MBTI focuses on each trait individually. But like the MBTI, no individual can ever have just one temperament. Almost every single person will have traits in all temperaments, so it would be extremely difficult to pinpoint just one category.

Overall, temperaments have the ability to give people a better sense of how they are and what they can do to change their personalities. Being a personality type merely tells someone how they are, but temperaments look beyond that surface-level interpretation. Temperament identification allows people to score themselves and potentially make a change for the better. They have more self-awareness about themselves and can better adapt if needed.

Both tests have the ability to yield useful information and at least give you a place to start from in analyzing someone. We turn to the last one of our personality tests in the Enneagram, which functions similarly to Keirsey's temperaments.

The Enneagram

The Enneagram test was developed in the 1960s as a way for people to attain *self-actualization*. It's a little different from the more stable, trait-based categories of previous personality models, because it paints a picture of human personality as a purposeful phenomenon, i.e., something that serves a particular function.

The focus is primarily on self-improvement because it forces people to face their own faults head-on. What makes it unique is that it aims to identify the *how* and *why* rather than the *what* people do. Rather than dive into the minutiae, it's helpful to have a broad overview of the types of possible outcomes from the Enneagram and try to spot yourself in them.

There are nine types that can be identified when taking this test.

Type One—The Reformer. These types of people are usually concerned with always being right and having a high level of integrity. They can also be deemed as being judgmental and self-righteous. Examples include priests and doctors.

Type Two—The Helper. These people have a yearning to be loved and appreciated. They are usually very generous but can also be seen as manipulative and prideful. Examples include mothers and teachers.

Type Three—The Achiever. These types of people love to be praised and applauded. They are workaholics, which can make them narcissistic and vain. Examples include actors and students.

Type Four—The Individualist. Typically, these types will search for meaning in their lives with a need to be unique. They are certainly creative but can also be moody and temperamental. Examples include musicians and painters.

Type Five—The Investigator. These people strive to be knowledgeable and competent. Most of the time, they are very objective, but they have the tendency to hoard themselves away. An example includes researchers.

Type Six—The Loyalist. These people are thoughtful in their planning and are very loyal to anyone they care about. They do question everything, and this can make them suspicious and paranoid. Examples include survivalists and police officers.

Type Seven—The Enthusiast. These types of people like adventure and are very energetic. They make the best of everything, and this can force them to be reckless and overindulgent. Examples include thrill-seekers and actors.

Type Eight—The Challenger. These people always have to be in control or have power. They are assertive, which can come off as aggressive and extreme. Examples include overbearing parents or people in the military.

Type Nine—The Peacemaker. Lastly, these people are stable and mediate situations. They're normally easygoing and accepting of all things. But this type of naive behavior can make them oblivious to negative things happening around them. Examples include hippies and grandparents.

Some people may exhibit a bit of each of these types, or be more dominant in just a few. It may be that you tend to exhibit one type in a certain context or environment, but switch to another when that context changes. Taking the test allows people to gain a better understanding of themselves and *why* they act the way they do in certain situations. By seeing human identity in terms of purpose, you can begin to see how personality becomes a tool with a particular function. The test also forces people to look at themselves in a deeper way that could potentially unlock more evolved and conscious ways of thinking.

Consider these personality tests the introduction to reading and analyzing people, because the process is as follows: understand various test scales, observe people, and then discern where people might fit. In the end, you might gain useful information, but you also might be trying to shoehorn people into incorrect categories or are overall wrong about your perception. From this point forward, we will focus more on individual observations and what they might say about people.

Takeaways:

- We start our journey into analyzing people like a psychologist by first taking a look at the various personality tests and seeing what we can glean from them. It turns out, quite a bit, although they can't be said to be definitive measures or categories of people. Mostly, they provide different scales and perspectives through which to view people differently.
- The Big Five personality traits are one of the first attempts to classify people based on specific traits rather than as a whole. You can remember the traits easily with the acronym OCEAN: openness to experience (trying new things), conscientiousness (being cautious and careful), extroversion (drawing energy from others and social situations), agreeableness (warm and sympathetic), and neuroticism (anxious and high-strung).
- Next, the MBTI, though helpful as a guideline, can sometimes suffer from people treating it like a horoscope and reading into their type what they wish to see about themselves. The MBTI functions on four distinct traits and how much of each trait you are or are not. The traits are generally

53

introverted/extroverted (your general attitude toward others), intuitive/feeling (how you perceive information), thinking/feeling (how you process information), and perceiving/judging (how you implement information). Thus, this creates 16 distinct personality types.

- The MBTI does suffer from some shortcomings, including the usage of stereotyping to classify people, and the lack of consistency when people score differently depending on their current moods and circumstances.

- The Keirsey temperaments are a way of organizing the same information gleaned from the MBTI. Here, there are four distinct temperaments, each with two types of roles instead of 16 personality types. The four temperaments are guardian, artisan, idealistic, and rational. Keirsey estimated that up to 80% of the population fell into the first two temperaments.

- Finally, the Enneagram is the final personality test we cover in this chapter. It is composed of nine general types of personalities: reformer, helper, achiever, individualist, investigator, loyalist, enthusiast, challenger, and peacemaker. Each type is composed of a specific set of traits, and in this way, it functions more similarly to Keirsey's temperaments.

Chapter 3. Open Your Eyes

The idea that people cannot help but reveal their true intentions and feelings one way or another is an appealing one. People can *say* whatever they like, but it's always been understood that "actions speak louder than words" and that people's facial expressions or body language can inadvertently reveal their deepest selves. We are in effect communicating all the time, sending out information about our intentions and feelings—but only a small fraction of this is verbal.

Observing people's actions and behavior in real-time is what we most commonly understand to be analyzing people. It might seem natural to look to people's physical bodies in space to intuit what's going on in their heads, and there's plenty of scientific evidence to support these claims. Physical appearance can tell you a lot about a person's feelings, motivations, and fears, even if they're actively trying to conceal these. In other words, the body doesn't lie!

Nevertheless, this approach to understanding people's motivations is not foolproof. When we're interacting with others and trying to understand what makes them tick, it's important to be cautious in making assumptions. We're all individuals, and context is very important. Though we can use various methods to read facial expressions and body language, it pays to remember that no single piece of information is enough to "prove" anything and that the art of reading people this way comes down to taking a holistic view of the full scenario as it unfolds in front of you.

Look at My Face

Have you ever felt a sudden hunch about how someone else was feeling? Maybe you had an instant sense that they felt a certain way (unhappy, fearful, angry, etc.), but if pressed you would not be able to say exactly why or how you came to this conclusion. Perhaps someone was smiling at you and yet you couldn't shake the feeling that they were angry; or perhaps somebody didn't say a word and yet it somehow *felt* like you knew exactly what they meant. What's going on behind all this?

Let's begin with Haggard and Isaacs in the 1960s. These researchers were interested in the role that facial expressions play in human communication. They filmed couples' faces during therapy and noticed little expressions that could only be caught when the film was slowed down. Later on, Paul Ekman expanded on his own theory on *microexpressions* and published a book, *Telling Lies*.

We all know how to read *macro*expressions—those facial movements that last up to four seconds in duration—but there are quicker, more fleeting expressions that are so fast they could easily be missed by the untrained eye. According to Ekman, facial expressions are actually physiological reactions. These expressions occur even when you're not around anyone who could see them. He found that across cultures, people used microexpressions to display their emotions on their faces in very predictable ways—even when they were attempting to conceal them or even when they themselves were unaware of the emotion.

His research led him to believe that microexpressions are spontaneous, tiny contractions of certain muscle groups that are predictably related to emotions and are the same in all people, regardless of upbringing, background, or cultural expectation. They can be as quick as one-thirtieth of a second long. But catching them and understanding what they mean is a way to cut through what is merely said to get to the deeper truth of what people feel and believe. Macroexpressions can be, to some extent, forced or exaggerated, but microexpressions are understood to be more genuine and difficult to fake or else suggestive of concealed or rapidly changing emotions.

Within the brain, there are two neural pathways related to facial expressions. The first is the *pyramidal tract*, responsible for voluntary expressions (i.e., most macroexpressions) and the *extrapyramidal tract* responsible for involuntary emotional facial expressions (i.e., microexpressions). Researchers have discovered that individuals who experience intense emotional situations but also external pressure to control or hide that expression will show activity in *both* these brain pathways. This suggests that they're working against one another, with the more conscious and voluntary expressions dominating the involuntary ones. Nevertheless, some tiny expressions of the real emotion may "leak" out—this is what you're looking for when you attempt to read a person in this way.

Incidentally, this may also be something you unconsciously pick up on sometimes. That person who is smiling at you, for example, may also briefly flash a microexpression of anger or annoyance–something you may still be able to register and feel, but only on an unconscious level. Remember that Haggard and Isaacs were only able to spot these tiny expressions when they slowed video recordings down.

So how, exactly, does one learn to read these expressions more *consciously*? Is it possible to capture these extremely tiny phenomena without using any sophisticated technology? Can you really decode a person's deepest feelings just by looking at a twitch of their nose or a wrinkle in their brow?

According to Ekman, yes–although as always, there are caveats. The basic understanding is that there are six universal human emotions, all with corresponding minuscule facial expressions. Happiness is seen in lifted cheeks, with the corners of the mouth raised up and back. Wrinkles appear under the eyes, between the upper lip and nose, and in the outside corner of the eyes. In other words, the movements we're all familiar with in an ordinary smile are there on a micro level too.

Microexpressions suggesting sadness are also what you'd expect. The outer corner of the eyes droops down, along with the corners of the lips. The lower lip may even tremble. Eyebrows may form a telltale triangle shape. For the emotion of disgust, the upper lip lifts and may be accompanied by wrinkles above it and wrinkles on the forehead. The eyes may narrow slightly as the cheeks are raised.

For anger, eyebrows lower and tense up, often at a downward angle. Eyes tighten, too, and the lips may be pursed or held stiffly open. The eyes are staring and piercing. Fear, on the other hand, entails similar contractions but upward. Whether open or closed, the mouth is tense, and both upper and lower eyelids are lifted. Finally, surprise or shock will show itself in elevated brows—rounded rather than triangular, like with sadness. The upper eyelids lift up and the lower eyelids stretch downward, opening the eyes wide. Sometimes, the jaw can hang loosely open.

As you can see, microexpressions are not very different from macroexpressions in the muscles that are involved; the main difference is in their speed, and to some extent their size. Ekman demonstrated, however, that these quick flashes of muscle contraction are so fast that people miss them: 99% of people they tested were unable to perceive them. Nevertheless, he also claims that people can be trained to look for microexpressions, and in particular learn to detect liars, a classic example of saying one thing and feeling another.

Ekman claims to be able to teach his technique within 32 hours, but for those of us who are curious about using the principles in our own lives, it's easy to start. Bear in mind, however, that although you can improve your accuracy, it's unrealistic to imagine that you could catch every single microexpression 100% of the time. We need to remember that most people have spent their lives mastering the art of concealing their raw, unfiltered emotional expression.

That said, there is always data to be gathered if you are observant enough. Firstly, a good rule of thumb is to look for discrepancies between what is said and what is actually demonstrated through facial expressions. For example, someone might be assuring you verbally and making promises but showing quick expressions of fear that betray their real position. They may be expressing anger, but on closer inspection, there are little flashes of the real emotion: sadness.

Spotting discrepancies will tell you when someone is trying to conceal what they really feel, and there may be many reasons for this concealment. One reason you may be particular interested in is the other person's intention to deceive. It is not so much that any single piece of body language conclusively reveals a lie; rather, it is the overall lack of cohesion in what is being presented. We are all used to looking for inconsistencies in the content of a lie, but pay attention also to irregularities in the way that content is presented.

Classic indicators that you are being lied to include lifting the shoulders slightly while someone is vehemently confirming the truth of what they're saying. Scratching the nose, moving the head to the side, avoiding eye contact, uncertainty in speaking, and general fidgeting also indicate someone's internal reality is not exactly lining up with the external—i.e., they might be lying.

It's worth mentioning here that this is not a foolproof method, and that research has mostly failed to find a strong relationship between body language, facial expression, and deceitfulness. Again, no single gesture alone indicates anything. Many psychologists have since pointed out that discrepancies in microexpressions can actually indicate discomfort, nervousness, stress, or tension, without deception being involved.

That said, we can make a note of that tension and become curious about what it means, and why it's happening. When used as a tool along with other tools, and when taken in context, microexpression analysis can be powerful. Granted, you'll need to stare quite intently at the person and observe them in a way that's uncomfortable and too obvious for normal social situations. You'll also have to weed out tons of irrelevant data and decide what gestures count as "noise" or meaningless idiosyncrasies.

At any rate, people who lack the required training have been shown to be astoundingly bad at spotting liars—despite feeling as though their gut intuitions about others' deceit is reliable. This means that even a slight increase in accuracy you might gain from understanding and implementing the microexpression theory may make all the difference. A microexpression may be small, but it's still a data point.

All this talk of unmasking liars may make this technique seem rather combative and underhanded, but Ekman is careful to point out that "lies" and "deceit," as he frames them, can also indicate the hiding of an emotion and not necessarily any malicious intent. There is certainly an allure in playing detective and uncovering people's secret feelings, but in reality, the use of microexpression analysis is a bit like CSI: it always looks a bit more impressive on TV than it is in real life.

Furthermore, the goal in developing the skill of microexpression analysis is not to play "gotcha!" to our friends and colleagues, but rather to enhance our own empathy and emotional intelligence, and to foster a richer understanding of the people around us. If we realize that someone is making considerable efforts to conceal their fear from us, for example, this knowledge can allow us to compassionately consider where they're coming from. It can encourage us to communicate in ways that won't further trigger their defensiveness, and to try and resolve the problem with kindness.

If you're not convinced about using microexpressions to detect deception, another perspective is not to look for lies or classify expressions according to their duration, but rather to look at what an expression typically conveys. Then, depending on context and how the expression compares to what's said *verbally*, you can come to your own conclusions.

Nervousness is typically behind things like tightening the lips or twitching the corners of the mouth very quickly toward the ear and back. Quivering lips or chin, a furrowed brow, narrowed eyes, and pulled-in lips may also indicate the person is feeling tense. If a person you know is normally calm and composed but you suddenly notice plenty of these little signs while they tell you a tale you don't quite believe, you might infer that, for some reason, they're nervous about telling it to you. Whether this is because they're lying or because their story is simply uncomfortable to tell—only you can decide from context.

A person feeling dislike or disagreement might purse their lips tightly, roll their eyes, flutter their eyelids briefly, or crinkle their nose. They may also squint a little or narrow their eyes like a cartoon villain staring down the hero, close their eyes, or "sneer" a little in a slight expression of disdain. If a person opens the Christmas present you gave them and immediately proceeds to do all of the above, you might want to assume they don't really like their gift, despite what they say to the contrary.

Those dealing with stress may find tiny ways to release that stress, giving themselves away even though for the most part they appear quite calm. Uncontrollable, fast blinking and making repetitive motions like twitching the cheek, biting the tongue, or touching parts of the face with their fingers can all indicate someone who's finding a particular situation stressful. This might make sense when someone's in a job interview or being questioned in connection with a crime but may be more noteworthy if you spot it in seemingly calm situations. This discrepancy gives you a clue that all might not be as it appears.

Pay attention also to asymmetry in facial expressions. Natural, spontaneous, and genuine expressions of emotion tend to be symmetrical. Forced, fake, or conflicting expressions tend not to be. If you can, try to watch a very young baby and observe the facial expressions they make. These are brand-new little humans who have not yet learnt to control their facial expressions or conceal their true emotions. Compare the spontaneous and authentic quality of these expressions with the deliberate artifice presented by, say, a celebrity on a talk show, or performer on stage. Can you see the difference? With practice, you may start to naturally recognize genuine expressions in your everyday interactions, and learn to distinguish them from deliberate and conscious facial movement.

Analyzing facial expressions is a powerful method of understanding others that's more than "skin-deep," but it's not foolproof. Try to interpret what you see in context, and consider the whole person, including any other body language they express. Every observation you make is simply a data point and doesn't prove anything either way. The skill comes in gathering as much data as you can and interpreting the whole, emerging pattern in front of you, rather than just one or two signs. For this reason, it's best to use what you know about microexpressions as a supplement to other methods and tools.

Body Talk

Body language, for instance, may be just as powerful a language to learn to read and comprehend as facial expressions. After all, the face is simply a part of the body. Why focus on just one part when people's postures and general movements can speak just as eloquently? Ex-FBI agent Joe Navarro is generally considered an authority in this field and has used his experience to teach others about the wealth of information people share without ever opening their mouths (i.e., what he calls "nonverbal communication").

Originally from Cuba and having to learn English after moving to the U.S. when he was eight years old, Navarro quickly came to appreciate how the human body was "a kind of billboard that advertised what a person was thinking." During his career he spoke at length about learning to spot people's "tells"—those little movements that suggest that someone is uncomfortable, hostile, relaxed, or fearful.

As with facial expressions, these tells may hint at deceit or lies but primarily indicate that someone is uncomfortable or that there is a discrepancy between what's felt and what's expressed. Armed with an understanding of how body language works, we can not only open up new channels on which to communicate with others, but pay attention to our own bodies and the messages we may be unwittingly sending to others.

Firstly, it's important to understand that nonverbal communication is inbuilt, biological, and the result of evolution. Our emotional responses to certain things are lightning-fast, and they happen spontaneously, whether we want them to or not. Importantly, they express themselves physically in the way we hold and move our bodies in space, potentially resulting in the transmission of thousands of nonverbal messages.

It's the more primitive, emotional, and perhaps honest part of our brain, the limbic brain, that's responsible for these automatic responses. While the prefrontal cortex (the more intellectual and abstract part) is a little removed from the body, and more under conscious control, it's also the part that's capable of lying. But even though a person can say one thing, their bodies will always speak the truth. If you can tune into the gestures, movements, postures, patterns of touching, and even the clothing a person wears, you give yourself a more direct channel into what they *really* think and feel. Navarro claims that the majority of communication is nonverbal anyway—meaning you're actively missing out on the bulk of the message by *not* considering body language.

Consider that communication started out nonverbally. In our earliest histories, before the development of language, humankind most likely communicated by gestures, simple sounds, and facial expressions. In fact, from the moment a baby is born it instinctively makes faces to communicate that it's cold, hungry, or frightened. We never need to be taught how to read basic gestures or understand tones of voice—this is because nonverbal communication was our first communication and may still be our preferred form.

Think of all the ways you already take nonverbal communication for granted—in the way you show love or demonstrate your anger. Even if you aren't aware of it, we are all still processing vast amounts of information on nonverbal channels. Learn how to read this information and you can determine if someone is trying to deceive you or perhaps if someone is trying to conceal their feelings and true intentions from you.

You've probably heard of the "fight-or-flight" response before, but there's a third possibility: freeze. What's more, these responses to danger may be quite subtle, but nevertheless, they speak to discomfort and fear. Our ancestors might have shown fight-or-flight when running from predators or enemy tribes, but those instincts might have followed us into the boardroom or classroom.

The limbic brain is again responsible for these fear responses. Someone who is asked a difficult question or put on the spot may look like a deer caught in headlights. They may lock their legs around a chair and stay fixed tight in that position (this is the freeze response). Another possibility is physically moving the body away from what is perceived as threatening. A person may put an object on their lap or position their limbs toward the exit (the flight response). Finally, a third person may "fight." This aggressive response to fear can show itself in picking arguments, verbally "sparring," or adopting threatening gestures.

In fact, the more competent you become at reading nonverbal signals, the more you may come to appreciate how fundamentally *physical* they are and how much they speak to our shared evolutionary history. In the past we might have literally fended off an attack with certain gestures or indeed set out to attack another with very obvious movements and expressions. These days, our world is very abstract and the things that threaten us are more verbal and conceptual—but the old machinery for expression, fear, aggression, curiosity, etc. is all still there, only perhaps expressed a little more subtly.

Let's consider what are called "pacifying behaviors." These can offer a key insight into someone who is feeling stressed, unsure, or threatened. Essentially, a pacifying behavior is what it sounds like—the (unconscious) attempt to self-soothe in the face of some perceived threat. When we feel stressed, our limbic brain may compel us to make little gestures designed to calm us: touching the forehead, rubbing the neck, fiddling with hair, or wringing the hands are all behaviors intended to soothe stress.

The neck is a vulnerable area of the body, but one that is relatively exposed. Consider how aggressive people "go for the jugular" and you understand how the throat and neck can be unconsciously felt to be an area open for fatal attack. It makes sense then that someone unconsciously covering or stroking this area is expressing their struggle, emotional discomfort, or insecurity. Men may use this gesture more often than women; men may fidget with their ties or squeeze the top of the neck, while women may put the fingers to the suprasternal notch (the indent between the collarbones) or play nervously with a necklace.

Pay attention to this behavior and you'll notice how it reveals someone's fears and insecurities in real-time. Someone might say something a little aggressive and another person responds by leaning back slightly, crossing the arms, and putting one hand up to the throat. Notice this in real-time and you can infer that this particular statement has aroused some fear and uncertainty.

Similarly, rubbing or touching the forehead or temples can signal emotional distress or overwhelm. A quick tap with the fingers may reveal a momentary feeling of stress, whereas a prolonged cradling of the head in both hands can spell extreme distress. In fact, you can consider any cradling, stroking, or rubbing movement as the physical clue of a person's need to self-pacify. This could mean touching cheeks when the person feels nervous or frightened, rubbing or licking the lips, massaging the earlobes, or running the fingers through the hair or beard.

Pacifying behaviors are not just things like stroking or rubbing, though. Puffing out the cheeks and exhaling loudly is also a gesture that releases considerable stress. Have you ever noticed how many people will do this after hearing bad news or narrowly escaping an accident? An unexpected stress release response is yawning—rather than indicating boredom, the body's sudden attempt to draw in more oxygen during stressful times is even seen in other animals. "Leg cleansing" is another, and it entails wiping down the legs as though to wash them or brush off dust. This can be missed if it's hidden under a table, but if you can notice it, it is a strong indication of an attempt to self-soothe during stressful moments.

"Ventilating" is another behavior you may not pay much attention to. Notice someone pulling their shirt collar away from their neck or tossing the hair away from the shoulders as though to cool off. They're likely experiencing discomfort or tension. Though this might be literally because of an uncomfortable environment, it's more likely a response to inner tension and stress that needs "cooling off."

One of the most obvious forms of pacifying behavior looks exactly like what a mother might do to a young child to soothe them: cradling and hugging one's own body or rubbing the shoulders as though to ward off a chill all suggest a person who feels under threat, worried, or overwhelmed—these gestures are an unconscious way to protect the body.

This is an important underlying principle across all of body language theory: that limbs and gestures may signal unconscious attempts to protect and defend the body. When you consider that the torso contains all the body's vital organs, you can understand why the limbic brain has reflex responses to shield this area when threats are perceived—even emotional threats.

Someone who is highly unresponsive to a request or who feels attacked or criticized may cross their arms as if to say, "Back off." Raising the arms to the chest during an argument is a classic blocking gesture, almost as if the words being exchanged were literally thrown, causing an unconscious reflex to fend them off. On a similar note, slumping, loose arms can indicate defeat, disappointment, or despair. It's as though the body is physically broadcasting the nonphysical sentiment of "I can't do this. I don't know what to do. I give up."

Let's take it further. Imagine someone standing over a desk, arms spread wide. Aren't you immediately reminded of an animal claiming territory? Wide, expansive gestures signal confidence, assertiveness, and even dominance. If a person is standing with arms akimbo, they leave their torso exposed. This is a powerful way to communicate that they are confident in taking up room and don't feel threatened or unsure in the least.

Other gestures of confidence and assertiveness include that favorite of politicians and businessmen the world over: "hand steepling." The fingertips are pressed together so they form a little steeple. It's the classic negotiating gesture, signaling confidence, poise, and certainty about your power and position, as though the hands were merely resting and calmly contemplating their next move.

On the other hand (pun intended) wringing and rubbing the hands is more likely to demonstrate a lack of feeling in control or doubt in one's own abilities. Again, this is a pacifying gesture designed to release tension. Hands are our tools to effect change in the world and bring about our actions. When we fidget, wring our hands, or clench our fists, we are demonstrating a lack of ease and confidence in our abilities or find it difficult to act confidently.

What about the legs? These are often overlooked since they might be concealed under a desk, but legs and feet are powerful indicators too. "Happy feet" can bounce and jiggle—on the other hand, bouncy legs paired with other nervous or pacifying gestures may indicate an excess of nervous tension and energy or impatience... or too much coffee, you decide. Toes that point upward can be thought of as "smiling" feet and indicate positive, optimistic feelings.

Physiologically, our legs and feet are all about, unsurprisingly, movement. Busy feet could suggest an unexpressed desire to get moving, either literally or figuratively! It's also been said that feet point in the direction they unconsciously wish to go. Both toes turned toward the conversation partner can signal "I'm here with you; I'm present in this conversation" whereas feet angled toward an exit could be a clue that the person really would prefer to leave.

Other clues that someone is wanting to move, leave, or escape are gestures like clasping the knees, rocking up and down on the balls of the feet, or standing with a bit of a bounce in the step—all of these subtly communicate someone whose unconscious mind has "fired up the engines" and wants to get going. This could mean they're excited about possibilities and want to get started as soon as possible, or they may have a strong dislike for the current situation and almost literally want to "run away." Again, context matters!

Legs and feet can also reveal negative emotions. Crossing the legs, as with the arms, can signal a desire to close off or protect the body from a perceived threat or discomfort. Crossed legs are often tilted toward a person we like and trust—and away from someone we don't. This is because the legs can be used as a barrier, either warding off or welcoming in someone's presence. Women may dangle shoes off the tips of the toes in flirtatious moments, slipping a shoe on and off the heel again. Without getting too Freudian about it, the display of feet and legs can indicate comfort and even intimacy with someone. On the other hand, locking the feet and ankles can be part of a freeze response when someone *really* doesn't like a situation or person.

So having discussed the face, hands, legs and feet, and torso in general, what else is there? Turns out, a lot more. The body as a whole can be positioned in space in certain ways, held in certain postures, or brought further or closer to other people. The next time you meet someone new, lean in to shake their hand and then watch what they do with their entire body.

If they "stand their ground" and stay where they are, they're demonstrating comfort with the situation, you, and themselves. Taking a step back or turning the entire torso and feet to the side suggests that you may have gotten too close for their comfort. They may even take a step closer, signaling that they are happy with the contact and may even escalate it further.

The general principle is pretty obvious: bodies expand when they are comfortable, happy, or dominant. They contract when unhappy, fearful, or threatened. Bodies move toward what they like and away from what they don't like. Leaning toward a person can show agreement, comfort, flirtation, ease, and interest. Likewise, crossing the arms, turning away, leaning back, and using tightly crossed legs as a barrier show a person's unconscious attempt to get away from or protect themselves from something unwanted.

Those people who spread out on public transport? They feel relaxed, secure, and confident (annoying, isn't it?). Those that seem to bundle themselves as tightly as possible may instead signal low confidence and assertiveness, as though they were always trying to take up less room. Similarly puffing up the chest and holding out the arms in an aggressive posture communicates, "Look how big I am!" in an argument, whereas raising the shoulders and "turtling" in on oneself is nonverbally saying, "Please don't hurt me! Look how small I am!"

We're not much like gorillas in the forest, beating our chests during heated arguments—

but if you look closely, you may still see faint clues to this more primal behavior anyway. Those postures that take up room and expand are all associated with dominance, assertiveness, and authority. Hands on the hips, hands held regally behind the back (doesn't it make you think of royalty or a dignified soldier who is unafraid of attack?), or even arms laced behind the neck as one leans back in a chair— all signify comfort and dominance.

When you are becoming aware of people's body language, ask in the first instance whether their actions, gestures, and postures are constricting or expanding. Is the face open or closed? Are the hands and arms spread wide and held loose and far from the body, or are the limbs kept close and tense? Is the facial expression you're looking at pulled tight or loose and open? Is the chin held high (sign of confidence) or tucked in (sign of uncertainty)?

Imagine you have no words at all to describe what you're looking at; just observe. Is the body in front of you relaxed and comfortable in space, or is there some tightness, tension, and unease in the way the limbs are held?

A lot of the art of body language is, once pointed out, rather intuitive. This is because each of us is actually already fluent in its interpretation. It is merely allowing ourselves to de-emphasize the verbal for a moment to take notice of the wealth of nonverbal information that's always flowing between people. None of it is really concealed. Rather, it's a question of opening up to data coming in on a channel we are not taught to pay attention to.

Putting It All Together

How can we use all of this to actually help us "read" people effectively and understand even those motivations, intentions, and feelings people may be actively trying to conceal? It's worth remembering right off the bat that detecting deception is not as straightforward as some would have you believe and, as we've seen, not as simple as spotting a telltale sign that proves a lie once and for all. Laypeople and professionals alike are notoriously bad at reading body language, despite the wealth of information we now have on the topic.

But the knack really comes in deciding what to do with certain observations once you've made them. Does a person's folded arms mean they're lying, unhappy about something, fearful... or just feeling cold? The trick comes in using not just one or two but a whole host of clues and tells to form a more comprehensive picture of behavior. The reason why it's so difficult to "spot a lie" with perfect accuracy is that the gestures and expressions associated with deception are often not different from those signifying stress or discomfort.

So given all this, is it worth learning to read body language? Absolutely. Adding this extra dimension to your interactions with others will only enrich your relationships and give you extra insight into your interpersonal conflicts and tensions. Knowing what's going on with another person allows you to be a better communicator and speak to what people are actually feeling rather than what they're merely saying.

Body language signals are always there. Every person is communicating nonverbally, at every moment of the day. And it is possible to not only observe this information in real-time but learn to properly synthesize and interpret it. You don't need to be an expert, and you don't need to be perfect. You just need to pay attention and be curious about your fellow human beings in a way you might not have before. As you're developing your body language reading skills, it may help to keep a few key principles in mind:

Establish normal behavior

One or two gestures in a conversation don't mean much. They could be accidental or purely physiological. But the more you know how someone "normally" behaves, the more you can assume that any behavior outside of this is worth looking more closely at. If someone *always* squints their eyes, pouts, jiggles their feet, or clears their throat, you can more or less discount these gestures.

Look for unusual or incongruent behavior

Reading people is about reading patterns of behavior. Pay special attention to clues that are unusual for that person. Suddenly fiddling with the hair and avoiding eye contact could tell you something is going on, especially if this person never does either of these things normally. You may with time come to recognize "tells" in people closest to you—they may always wrinkle their nose when being dishonest or clear their throat excessively when they're afraid and pretending not to be.

Importantly, pay close attention to those gestures and movements that seem incongruous. Discrepancies between verbal and nonverbal communication can tell you more than merely observing nonverbal communication alone. It's about context. An obvious example is someone wringing their hands, rubbing their temples, and sighing loudly but who claims, "I'm fine. Nothing's wrong." It's not the gestures that tell you this person is concealing distress, but the fact that they're incongruent with the words spoken.

Gather plenty of data

As we've seen, certain constricting behaviors could merely be because one is cold, tired, or even ill, and expansive gestures may not be about confidence so much as feeling physically warm and wanting to cool off. This is why it's important to never interpret a gesture alone. Always consider clusters of clues.

If you see something, note it but don't come to any conclusions immediately. Look to see if they do it again. Look for other gestures that may reinforce what you've seen or else give evidence for the opposite interpretation. Check to see if the behavior repeats itself with other people or in other contexts. Take your time to really *analyze* the whole of what's in front of you.

Look for mirroring

An important thing to remember is that certain gestures may mean one thing in one context or when shown to one person but have a different meaning in another context or with someone else. In other words, certain gestures could literally only apply to you as you speak to this person. If you're not very familiar with someone, a quick body language–reading shortcut is to merely notice whether they are or are not mirroring your gestures, whatever they are.

Mirroring is a fundamental human instinct; we tend to match and mimic the behavior and expressions of those we like or agree with, while we don't if we dislike a person or perceive them negatively. If you're in a meeting with a new client, you may notice that no matter how friendly your voice or how often you smile and make open-handed, warm gestures, they respond with coldness and closed gestures, failing to mirror back to you your optimism. Here, the gestures themselves are irrelevant; it's the fact that they are not shared which shows you that the person you're dealing with is unreceptive, hostile, or threatened.

Pay attention to energy

This is not some fluffy, esoteric idea: in a group, simply take note of where intention, effort, and focus are being concentrated. Watch where energy flows. Sometimes, the "leader" of a group is only so in name; the real power may lie elsewhere. One only needs to look at how much focus and attention flows toward a baby in the room to see this in action—the baby says and does very little yet nevertheless commands the attention of everyone there. Similarly, a family may have the father as the official "leader," and he may gesture and talk loudly to cement this perception. But pay attention and you may see that it's his wife who is constantly deferred to, and every member of the family may show with their body language that it is in fact their mother's needs that take precedence, despite what's claimed verbally.

The most powerful voice in a room is not necessarily the loudest. A lot can be understood about the power dynamics in a group by watching to see where energy flows. Who speaks the most? Who are people always speaking *to*, and how? Who always seems to take "center stage"?

Remember that body language is dynamic

When we speak, the content of our language isn't just about the words and the grammar we use to string them together. It's about *how* we talk. Do we say a lot or a little? What tone of voice? Are sentences long and complicated or short and terse? Is everything phrased tentatively, like a question, or is it stated confidently, as though it's a known fact? What's the speed of delivery? How loud? Is it clear or mumbling?

In the same way that verbal information can vary in the way it's communicated, nonverbal information can vary too. Gestures are not static, fixed things but living expressions that move in time and space. Watch the flow of information in real-time. Watch how expressions change and move in response to the environment and those in it. Don't be curious about "catching" a discreet gesture, but rather watch the flow of gestures as they change.

For example, look at how a person walks. Walking is like a body posture but set in motion. Shuffling, slow gaits suggest lack of confidence, while springy, quick ones suggest optimism and excitement. Become interested in how a person responds to others in conversation or their style of talking to those in positions of power. Once you start looking, you'll be amazed at the wealth of information that's just waiting there to be noticed.

Context is everything

Finally, it bears repeating: no gesture occurs in a vacuum. Nonverbal communication needs to be considered in relation to everything else— just like verbal communication. Establish patterns and learn about a person's behavior over time, in different contexts, and toward different people. Consider the situation and environment—sweating and stuttering during your wedding vows or a big interview is understandable; doing so when asked to explain what you're doing snooping through someone's drawers is a little more suspicious.

Remember that everyone has their own unique, idiosyncratic personality. Factor into your analysis the fact that people are either introverted or extroverted, may favor emotions or intellect, may have high or low tolerance for risk and adversity, may thrive in stressful situations or wither in them, and may be spontaneous and casual or goal-directed and rather serious. Our instinctual, evolutionarily programmed impulses can't be hidden or resisted, but they can take on slightly different forms depending on our unique personalities.

Admittedly, reading facial expressions and body language is a skill that takes time and patience to master. There are no quick and easy tricks to understanding people's deeper motivations. However, remember the above principles and focus on honing your powers of observation, and you'll soon develop a knack for seeing and understanding even tiny ripples and flutters of behavior you might have previously missed. We live in a world dominated by words and language. But when you become a student of nonverbal communication, it's no exaggeration to say that you open yourself up to an entirely different, sometimes quite strange world.

It's all in the Eyes

Everyone's heard that the eyes are the window to the soul, but it turns out that this old saying may be more grounded in fact than we realize. A fairly recent study by Sabrina Hoppe and colleagues explored the relationship between eye movements and personality traits.

The 2018 paper, titled *Eye Movements During Everyday Behavior Predict Personality Traits,* was published in *Frontiers in Human Neuroscience.* The team closely monitored the eye movements of 42 study participants as they went about their day on a university campus. They also assessed their personality traits using standard psychological inventories and questionnaires.

The research was thorough, with the team tracking metrics such as blink rate, pupil size, fixation duration (how long someone stared at any one particular object), and saccade amplitude (meaning the distance the eyes travel between two fixed points and back again). Based on their eye movement data alone, the team was able to successfully predict the participants' scores on , the Big 5 personality traits-neuroticism, extraversion, agreeableness, conscientiousness, and openness to experience.

The researchers found that neuroticism was associated with higher blink rate, bigger pupil size, and longer fixation duration. Extraversion was associated with lower blink rate, smaller pupil size, and longer saccades, and so on.

This finding is a pretty big deal: it suggests that it really is possible to discern someone's personality simply by watching their eye movements. It tells us that an individual's personality is so pervasive that it even influences the subtle movement of their eyes—in other words, the eyes can be considered their own form of micro body language.

Further research may uncover even more links between personality, eye movement, mood, thought processes, and behavior. The study authors note that their results pose interesting questions for new concepts in marketing, psychometrics, and even human-machine interfacing and AI (i.e., using computers to quickly ascertain human personality).

It's important to note that this study was rather small, and as such there are obvious limitations as well as ethical concerns about privacy and how such findings may be used. What's more, the team's methodology was never able to predict personality with 100% accuracy–in fact, accuracy varied somewhat according to the traits measured, with extraversion being the highest (48.6% accuracy) and openness to experience the lowest (30.8%). Again, we see that no single data point allows us to pinpoint a person's personality with complete precision; we always need to consider the bigger picture, and gather as much data as possible.

Another thing to consider is that the research was conducted using sophisticated machine-learning algorithms and other high-tech tools. The eye movement tracking conducted by the researchers was not the kind of thing you do in everyday conversation! Most mere mortals will not be able to note, for example, the millisecond differences between eye saccades or blink rate.

That said, *can* we apply some of the general findings of the study to our own everyday interactions? Let's take a look at the Big 5 personality traits and the patterns of eye movement most commonly associated with each. Bear in mind that these are very broad, high-level categories. We can imagine that every personality is a unique mix of varying amounts of these different key "ingredients." The more you understand about each trait, the more you can see how its characteristic eye movements are a natural expression of that state of mind.

Neuroticism

What it is: This is the trait that underlies moodiness and overall emotional instability. Neuroticism is fundamentally a stress response to what a person perceives as a threat. It's about someone's ability to cope with stress and risk. High levels of neuroticism manifest as anxiety, irritability, and overthinking, while low levels indicate more emotional stability. People with low levels of neuroticism tend live more easily in the present. They also generally don't experience prolonged depression and anxiety.

How to spot it: Given neuroticism's link with threat, stress, and anxiety, look for eye movements that are erratic and show high variability. High neuroticism will reveal itself in restless, rapid eye movements and variable eye pupil size–this is a hint of the mental busyness happening on the inside!

Extraversion

What it is: Classically, extraversion (or extroversion, as it's sometimes known) is the trait of being energized, rather than drained, by social situations. High extraversion, then, is about energy that is projected and expanded outwards beyond the self, and includes being expressive, talkative, and curious. Introversion, on the other hand, is a tendency for attentional energy to turn inwards, manifesting in more time spent on solo pursuits, and more time in introspection. . Low extraversion is characterized by a more retreating stance, quietness, and reservation. These are people that may respond well to others, but only if they are the ones to approach first.

How to spot it: It follows, then, that high extraversion "eye body language" will reflect this external orientation. Look for stable, focused eye movements and, when the eyes shift, a tendency for them to do so deliberately. The eyes will tend to focus on social cues and people, rather than the inanimate environment. High extraversion is about eyes that seem to be seeking eye contact; low extraversion will have eye movement that is more evasive and private.

Agreeableness

What it is: Broadly speaking, high agreeableness correlates to kindness, trust, affection, and other pro-social behaviors like cooperating and sharing. Those scoring low agreeableness are less ready to accommodate others. They are less empathetic, lack interest in people, and are unwilling to conform or compromise.

How to spot it: This trait may be a little trickier to recognize through eye movements alone. Look for relaxed, calm eye movements and the tendency to fixate on faces and other aspects of social situations. This indicates a person who is gathering data about what is happening with others, so that they can, essentially, harmonize with them. Conversely, eye movements that seem unsettled and relatively uninterested in people or social dynamics reveal less of an interest in being agreeable.

Conscientiousness

What it is: A conscientious person is one who has the drive to do their duty well and follow the standards of their own conscience. High conscientiousness is fundamentally about deliberate control and self-management, and so it reveals itself as good impulse control, goal-directed behavior, and a certain level of organization and structured thinking. Highly conscientious types plan well and do their job, whereas those with low conscientiousness tend to be unorganized, unstructured, and undisciplined.

How to spot it: Thinking in terms of self-management and control, it's obvious that those low in conscientiousness will exhibit lower control over their eye movements, which could be more disorganized overall. Pay close attention to how people respond to random interruptions. Conscientious people show more consistency and attention to detail–literally, their eyes will notice and take in small details.

Openness to experience

What it is: This is the human tendency to want to learn, experience new things, and explore. It's the personality trait associated with curiosity, novelty, and interest. High openness correlates with creativity and even willingness to take risks, whereas low openness is about staying a little more in one's comfort zone with a more tried-and-true, traditional approach.

How to spot it: Openness to experience manifests itself as an overall perceptual curiosity about the world. People with high openness tend to use their eyes in an exploratory way–there are frequent gaze shifts, and varied fixation points. These are eyes that are always scanning with interest, always exploring–"learning eyes". Conversely, lower openness may reveal itself in a more stable, unvarying gaze that is not as interested in the surrounding perceptual landscape.

The eyes are a window to the soul precisely because they are an *external* indicator of certain *internal* processes that are ordinarily hidden from view. The eyes are often a person's dominant sense organ, and they are used to gather information and navigate the world in a very idiosyncratic way. If we can watch what someone is doing with their eyes, we can get a glimpse into what they may be doing with their minds, their imaginations, and their emotions.

Watch someone's eyes and you see what they are paying attention to, and what they are ignoring; this tells you a tiny bit about their goals, their values, and their priorities, even if only in that particular context. Watch the style of eye movement (the energy and expression) and you can get an inkling of overall anxiety levels.

In the same way as our body language can be either expansive or constricted, so can our eye gaze. We can look on something or someone with the intention of connecting with it, or reaching out to encounter it. We can also use our gaze to observe something, but keep it at a distance, i.e., we appraise a threat, or we take note of a stimulus without necessarily involving ourselves in it.

Learning to read the eyes is an art, but we now have the science to support what many of us have intuitively known for a long time. To summarize, the next time you're in a social situation, take a close look at how someone is using their eyes. Ask yourself:

- Is the gaze stable or rapidly shifting all over the place?
- Is the gaze diffuse, or does it fixate on certain things? What kind of things?
- Is the gaze relaxed and calm or energetic and restless?
- Is the gaze social or more focused on non-human elements in the environment?
- Is the gaze expansive or constricted? Does it turn outwards or inwards?

Bearing in mind that even sophisticated machine-learning tools were not able to be 100% accurate in their appraisals, remember that your own accuracy will also depend heavily on how much data you can gather, as well as how much additional contextual information you're able to factor into your reading. In this respect, you are probably many times more accurate than the algorithms!

Takeaways:

- Finally, we get right into the thick of it. How can we read and analyze people just through sight and observation? We cover two primary aspects: facial expressions and body language. It's important to note that though many aspects have been scientifically proven (with physiological origins), we can't say that simple observations are foolproof. It can never be definitive because there are too many external factors to take into account. But we can better understand what typical things to look for and what we can glean from them.

- We use two types of facial expressions: micro- and macroexpressions. Macroexpressions are larger, slower, and more obvious. They are also routinely faked and consciously created. Microexpressions are the opposite of all of those things: incredibly quick, almost unperceivable, and unconscious. Psychologist Paul Ekman identified a host of microexpressions for each of the six basic emotions and in particular has also identified microexpressions to indicate nervousness, lying, or deception.
- Body language has a much broader range of possible interpretations. Generally, a relaxed body takes up space, while an anxious body contracts and wants to conceal and comfort itself. There are too many specifics to list in a bullet point, but just keep in mind that the only true way to analyze body language is to first know exactly what someone is like when they are normal.
- Eyes have a body language all their own; pay attention and you may spot hints about

someone's overall personality.Pay attention to the stability, direction, energy, and expression of the gaze, and what this implies about a person's inner processes

Chapter 4. Emotional Cues

When it comes to reading and analyzing people, this chapter is where we truly begin to delve into observations and how we can interpret them. It's where we start to practically apply all the theory we've covered so far and put it to good use.

Now, that's not to say that the previous chapters are not extremely useful; however, they are best understood as groundwork and foundation. Now is the time to remind ourselves of our initial goal, which is to take a (brief) look at someone and instantly get a good idea of their deeper traits, hopes, dreams, and overall mindset.

The categorical models we've already explored tell us a lot about what people *are*. In this chapter, however, we'll be trying to figure out who people are by understanding what they *feel*. Learning to spot and decode emotional cues is a big part of mastering the art of people-reding.

Analyzing others is hopefully intertwined with self-awareness, and that's where we begin by looking at the individual components of emotional intelligence and how it helps us read others.

Emotional Genius

The best modern conception of emotional intelligence arguably comes from psychologist Daniel Goleman.

According to Goleman and the many thinkers and theorists inspired by his work, Emotional Intelligence (or EQ) is knowing and perceiving the emotions you feel and why you feel them, then transferring that type of awareness onto others. This is the self/others interplay we mentioned in our opening chapter. Emotional Intelligence is not a trait so much as a two-step process: you are able to put a label on your *own* emotional state and accurately determine its cause and effect. If you're able to understand your own emotional situations accurately, you'll be able to read and understand others'.

When you start thinking "Why did she say that?" and "What made him do that?" instead of immediately reacting, that's the beginning of your path to emotional intelligence. It's a matter of understanding the whole causal chain of other people's motivations and intentions and how that leads to their emotions, which lead to their behaviors. We can think of emotional intelligence as a form of *empathetic imagination*–it's a way to understand the worlds of others through our own.

People who are emotionally intelligent find that the domain their intelligence plays out in is the social and emotional world. High EQ means not only knowing that this emotional world exists, but also knowing its rules and patterns, and knowing how to navigate its dangers and opportunities successfully. Viewed from the outside, high emotional intelligence can look like being able to read someone's mind. In reality, this everyday superpower is not so complex, and only requires a little open-mindedness and the willingness to resist focusing on ourselves all the time!

Take Charlotte. Charlotte prances into the office one day, a bounce in her step and a smile on her face. Before sitting down, she asks her coworker a question: "What do you think of my new haircut?" Derek, her coworker, doesn't care what her hair looks like whatsoever, but he likes Charlotte, and he also knows that she often worries about her looks. "It looks great," he enthuses. "The new cut really brings out your eyes."

"I thought so too!" she gushes, taking her seat. "Thanks." She smiles.

Because Derek understood and cared about Charlotte's emotions, he knew she was asking for encouragement and praise rather than an apathetic dismissal. He read the situation and connected to her emotional state rather than to her simple and seemingly innocent question. His emotional intelligence allowed him to grasp the deeper nature of the situation, and the real emotional need behind Charlotte's question. His kind response bolstered her impression of his trustworthiness and kindness, raising her opinion of him. It's a tiny thing, yes, but it's smart. It's the kind of people-reading skill that can dramatically change the world you live in.

Every time you improve your emotional intelligence, you'll have more interactions like these. It's about understanding and consideration and stepping outside of your own desires and perspectives. A less emotionally intelligent man would simply think, "What? It's just a haircut. Haircuts don't mean anything." But this is, again, a lack of empathetic imagination–the ability to step outside of one's own emotional perspective and voluntarily enter into someone else's. The less emotionally intelligent person lacks not only compassion, but also a certain breadth and depth of understanding.

Obviously, this goes a lot further than workplace niceties. Daniel Goleman's modern conception of emotional intelligence is a great place to start developing a better understanding of the nuances and complexities of this type of intelligence. His theory can be organized into four major categories, all of which work together to create a blueprint for understanding and reading others more effectively.

Self-Awareness

When we're self-aware, we know who we are, what we think, and what we feel. We know that when we get depressed, we'll get less done. We know that when we drink coffee, we tend to be peppier and more productive. We understand that when we're feeling stressed, we're less likely to have patience for other people's needs. We recognize emotion as an underlying basis for most of our actions.

In short, we have knowledge of what we feel, why we feel that way, and how our feelings will impact our behavior. Self-aware people are also able to observe the effects their emotions have on other people. Happiness and sadness alike tend to be contagious, and a self-aware person will know that their emotions impact and are impacted by their environment.

Self-awareness also involves knowing our strengths and knowing our weaknesses. More importantly, it helps us be willing and able to accept advice and criticism. People who aren't as aware of their real skills or value will either think they're too incompetent and incapable of learning or that they already know everything and don't need to be taught.

Neither is true of anyone, and people who fall into those traps come off as lazy or as arrogant know-it-alls, respectively. When you can admit you need help and accept the help or advice offered, you show other people that you value their opinion and respect their knowledge. Accepting help makes the people helping you feel important and needed, which is something we all appreciate. Stop thinking about your faults as bad things; they're really opportunities to make friends and learn new things.

You can improve your self-awareness in a lot of ways. Overall, you just need to know yourself better. Professional-level psychological or personality tests can give some insight, as can asking your friends to rate you on various personality traits or skills. It's also possible to watch how people respond to you when you do or say certain things and gain insight about what traits you have that contribute to their reactions.

Or you can simply sit and reflect upon things you've done and ask *why*. And then ask *why* again. And then do it three more times—this typically allows you to cut through the defenses you've constructed around yourself and get to the heart of matters. Anything that gives you feedback about why you feel your emotions is useful.

Take a step back and pause whenever you experience a strong emotion. Close your eyes and try to trace what happened in the past hour or two that led you to feel that way. Are there any facts or experiences in the past that would explain why you feel a particular way about certain things and people in your life? What is currently casting a subconscious shadow over your mood?

For example, if you're angry at 6:00 p.m., start thinking about what you've done since 3:00 p.m. You've driven home, had a snack, changed into your sweatpants, and watched a little bit of television.

When you visualize your drive home, though, suddenly you remember that you were cut off by somebody and that you were beeped at incessantly. This agitated you and you were still feeling the effects of that mood dampener hours later. This is a simplification of the process that begins to take place much more instantly.

The sad reality is that most people are not in tune with their feelings. Often, we are negatively affected by the emotional impact of things that have long since been irrelevant. Most people just react automatically without realizing why and without stopping to think what is happening internally. They fall into patterns that are sometimes negative and sometimes destructive.

Rather than looking inward and attempting to label your emotions based on what you might hypothesize caused them, you can also analyze how you are acting and label them that way. In the former, you are looking to the past to try to deduce a cause. In the latter, you are looking at the present to see the manifestation of emotion. In a sense, you are working backward from what you see and creating at least one theory about what caused it.

Just as with other people, you can tell more about yourself by your actions than you can by what you say (or what you tell yourself).

Self-Management

The most fundamental aspect of self-management is the ability to keep our emotions in check. When we're ecstatic because we got a date with a dreamboat, we don't let that excitement distract others in business meetings. When we're angry about being overlooked for a promotion, we don't let that impact our work relationship with our rival or our boss.

We even work to stay calm, steady, and effective when situations are stressful, hostile, or dangerous. In short, it involves not letting emotions get the best of you. It's about control and having the maturity to self-regulate. For example, you get up in the morning, and you realize that you're feeling cranky and a little under the weather. You don't instantly get out of bed, yell at the dog, and decide that the cause of all your life's problems is that someone left their socks on the floor. Instead, you have the presence of mind to think, "Hm, I'm cranky today." then decide to control, regulate, and correct that feeling. Realizing you might be coming down with a cold, you take a painkiller and some extra vitamins, you keep warm, and you make plans to take things a little easier that day. You manage your feelings and by doing so, you claim ownership over them.

A lot of people attempt to do this in a maladaptive way: by bottling up their emotions. That's a bad idea because it can lead to resentment, bitterness, and even eventual explosions of hatred and rage. Our emotions help us understand what we really think about events and people. Paying attention to them can let us form rational descriptions of our concerns and joys that can let us impact our work and relationships in positive ways. Notice what you feel, examine why you feel it, and talk about it calmly with relevant parties when your head is clear. That will let you form meaningful compromises and help you gain more happiness in life. In short, express emotions in appropriate, productive ways; don't repress them. This step is the next step in being self-aware: what do you actually *do* with your emotions that you've identified?

Self-management also involves monitoring our thoughts and moods to manufacture a positive outlook. Some people are natural optimists, some aren't, but seeking out the opportunities and lessons in even the worst situations can produce a silver lining that allows for meaningful growth and progress. You can't let yourself be crushed by a failure; you have to push through it, learn everything it taught you by heart, and do better next time. A well-managed emotional life is used to motivate you toward your goals because you can use conscious patterns of optimistic thought to rally yourself with hope and joy, letting you continue on your journey. Everyone likes people who can encourage them to go on in the face of hardship, and developing this optimism will do exactly that.

The final trait in self-management is flexibility. A lot of people become attached to doing things a certain way and balk when a better method comes along. Others are so scared of change that they presume anything new must be bad. But a self-managed person will see those impulses as unhelpful and try to learn new ways of thinking and doing things. This helps them adapt and manage their expectations and emotions better.

Self-Motivation

Arguably a subset of self-management, self-motivation pushes people to meet and exceed expectations—because they know what emotions they want more and less of. They have a good guess on what will make them feel fulfilled, and they try to accomplish that constantly. They take responsibility for themselves and follow an internalized code of self-control–i.e., a belief that their mindset and attitude play a big part in what happens to them in life.

Self-motivated people continually look for ways to improve their emotional state. They know what makes them tick, emotionally and otherwise, and try to set themselves up for success. You can supercharge your ability to do this by noticing when you or others complain. Complaints indicate problems, which are opportunities for improvement. When you find these, think about ways to solve the problem, and when you can make those solutions happen, get to it!

Social Awareness

People who are socially aware can read the room and understand the emotions that groups and individuals are likely feeling.

At a group level, being socially aware means understanding the power structure and organization of groups, along with the emotional impact of those structures and the emotional currents that flow between one person and the next. Social awareness helps us interpret social situations. Understanding that the secretary is happy to help her boss, but is tired from overwork, is part of social awareness.

It's also social awareness to know that she's more replaceable and therefore less important, and that both she and her boss are influenced by that dynamic. It's social awareness to notice and understand the significance of the friendly but curt tone of voice the boss takes, as well as the function of the laughter or silence of the secretary as they have a difficult budget conversation. It sounds like an overwhelming amount of data to process, but it can be simplified. Ask why people have certain behaviors with one person versus another, and then become curious about the dynamic that cause those behaviors.

As you can imagine, one cannot begin to have social awareness is they don't first have… awareness. One ironic and unfortunate side-effect of social anxiety, shyness, or self-consciousness is that it might impair a person's ability to pay full attention to the social world around them. In other words, if a person is too engrossed with themselves in social situations, they may not be able to fully recognize and absorb the ocean of social data flowing around them. This means they can't react to it, and ultimately become even more disconnected.

There is sometimes a self-fulfilling prophecy with people who worry about how they come across in social situations. For example, the person who is constantly worrying, "Do people like me?", is not sufficiently socially aware to respond and engage with others in the moment. They fail to notice nuances and don't follow subtle cues. In time, this really could lead to others not liking them!

There is hope, though, even if you've found it difficult in the past to fully immerse yourself in social dynamics. Observing and interacting with people helps develop the skill of social awareness. Whenever you see an interaction that puzzles or intrigues you, you can ask yourself *why* they're saying and doing what they are, to try to get a better grasp of relationship dynamics. The better you get, the easier it will be to find the right things to do in social situations of every size and type. One good side effect is that this will probably make you less anxious.

Obviously, this is a massive oversimplification, but much of social awareness begins with simply asking why something is happening, and what unseen or unconscious elements are causing it. It's nothing more than a willingness to direct your awareness outside of yourself, and to become curious about all the things you discover there.

Ask yourself these questions, one at a time at first, and very quickly it will become instinctual habit. You'll find yourself automatically thinking along these lines and the process will become more natural to you.

Of course, each situation is different, and you must be adaptable in discovering why people feel what they do. Don't be in too much of a hurry to answer your own question. Stay curious and open-minded, and don't lean too much on your own assumptions and prejudices. Going through the following checklist will assist you in reading people's emotions in a way you may never have considered before.

- How might your thoughts and actions be misinterpreted?
- What are other people's primary motivations and what unspoken, underlying motivations might they have that they (and you) are not even aware of?
- Consider people's built-in biases and life circumstances that give rise to certain emotions. What is their background and upbringing?
- How do people display their emotions both positively and negatively?
- How are emotions displayed in different ways?
- What emotions are they likely to be feeling and why?
- What is the purpose for what they are saying?
- What is their baseline emotional state and preferred interaction style?

By being aware of these factors, you increase your emotional intelligence because you are able to read people more accurately. And just as important, you can respond to them in a more calibrated manner that leads to fewer negative reactions. Notably, this process can take a while—exactly the difference between responding and reacting.

At the most basic level, emotional intelligence is knowing the range of reactions to any given statement or circumstance and who might respond differently and why.

If you insult someone's mother in a serious manner and with a serious face, one reaction would be anger and being offended. You can expect that reaction a majority of the time. However, what are the other possible reactions, and what accounts for the difference? People might assume you are joking, laugh out of confusion, or ignore you because they didn't even hear what you said.

Emotional intelligence will allow you to connect with people on a deeper level because you understand them implicitly without their saying anything. You will just get them. This is what many people interpret as chemistry and rapport, and you will have it in a seemingly effortless manner.

You can see how emotional intelligence starts from yourself and then transfers to others. In the previous chapter, we focused a lot on values and deeper intentions, which inform how people would like to act. Here, we are paying more attention to emotions, which tells you how people will naturally and instinctually act. Taken together, we are learning how to analyze someone's rational and emotional sides to both predict their behavior and also interpret it.

Another vital aspect of social awareness is learning to recognize and discern the subtext of an interaction or situation. For this, we'll need to learn the ins and outs of communication.

That's Not What I Meant!

Communication is so much more than the words that we speak or hear. Studies have quoted figures stating that 50% to 90% of communication—the message and emotion we get from others—is based on nonverbal or unspoken signals. Mehrabian and Ferris first noted this surprising statistic in "Inference of Attitudes from Nonverbal Communications in Two Channels" way back in 1967, and ever since then researchers have continued to find evidence supporting the significance of nonverbal communication. Add that to additional communication based on subtext, context, implication, and inference, and you'll almost wonder what impact our actual words have!

Whatever the case, what we think we are communicating is often overshadowed or outright contradicted by what is meant to be interpreted between the lines. What we say is not really what we mean most of the time, and this is something we begin to learn as children. It's not that the words we use don't matter— they do. But the way in which we use them, and the contexts we use them in, are far more indicative of our feelings and emotions.

Unfortunately, for many of us, these small signs might as well be incantations for magic spells based on how subtle or convoluted they seem. One of the keys to communicating more clearly and being able to read between the lines of what people say is to understand *subtext*. To borrow from Chaney and Lyden's 1997 publication "Subtextual Communication Impression Management: An Empirical Study," in the context of an office environment, subtext is the following:

> Subtextual communication, a covert language that strengthens or negates the spoken text, is used to influence the impressions other people have of us and may be used to competitive advantage in numerous situations in the workplace.

The subtext is more subtle than the obvious text and may be more honest in interactions between people (Fast, 1991).

Subtextual communication elements are related to image and may convey positive or negative impressions related to assurance, credibility, competence, and savoir-faire through dress, manner of introducing people, body language, regard for time, use of electronic communication, and dining etiquette.

Paul got a part-time job to give him extra cash as he earned his university degree. He decided to work in a local electronics store because he knew the people, the area, and the product like the back of his hand. Imagine his surprise when he discovered he wasn't the big sales star he made himself out to be during the interview process.

Everyone else seemed to hit their sales quotas with ease, yet there he was, stuck barely reaching the lower end of the target. What made matters worse was the fact that other staff members had absolutely no technical knowledge, yet they surpassed Paul in sales every single month.

Paul's sales were so bad that his boss called him in for a performance meeting to address the problem. Instead of pointing out where Paul went wrong, he decided to match him up with his top salesman to discover how the sales techniques differed.

For the entire afternoon, Paul tagged along with the top-performing salesperson, Sam. As Paul observed, he noticed something interesting. The customers were all completely the same, the queries were all the same, and his solutions were the same—except for one small thing.

Where Paul would give up or move on, Sam offered additional recommendations and moved in for the kill. He realized this when a customer was looking at a camera. The customer raised his hands and declared the product to be "fine." At this point, Sam picked up a more expensive camera and walked the customer through its features. Paul wouldn't usually do that—when the customer said something was "fine," he would continue focusing on closing the sale on the same camera.

But to his surprise, the customer ended up buying the more expensive camera. As soon as the customer left the store, Paul asked Sam, "What made you suggest a whole new product?

Isn't that just confusing the customer? I thought he said it was fine!"

Sam just laughed and said, "Just because the customer says it's fine doesn't mean it is. Fine is not positive. It usually means they want something more or their expectations haven't been met. It's them asking for more options in reality."

Paul was taking people's words literally and only at face value, and because of that, he was missing the real messages people were sending him. Whatever was being said was the only thing Paul was operating on, and he didn't consider that communication would occur in any other way.

Sam explained that people's words were merely the tip of the iceberg in terms of what they wanted to communicate, and "fine" said with a flat speaking tone was as good as "this sucks." That one simple statement made a huge change in Paul's sales, as he began trying to dig beneath the words themselves and pick up on the meaning behind them.

Don't be like Paul. Learn subtext to read people better and begin to respond to what people are truly trying to communicate.

Communication can be divided into two categories: overt and covert. Overt is the words we say and the explicit messages we want to convey. This is when we directly tell someone that we're hungry and ask for a hamburger. Covert, on the other hand, is what is meant, implied, insinuated, or suggested indirectly.

Subtext is an example of covert communication. It's almost never directly said, relies on literally anything besides the direct message coming out of someone's mouth, and requires correct interpretation. Using subtext to say "I'm hungry" would include rubbing your stomach, licking your lips, pointing out that there is a menu on a nearby table, and mentioning that your previous meal was tiny.

Not everyone is going to pick up on those signs, but it is undeniable what the person wanted to convey. We routinely communicate through these indirect means and hope that it saves us the trouble of being direct. Subsequently, understanding the subtext under and surrounding people's seemingly benign statements gives you insight into their true feelings and thoughts.

For example, how does the overt dialogue below differ from the subtextual, covert message? Here, it's what is *not said* that completes the message. The subtext is that the question wasn't replied to in a convincing manner and, thus, is less than sincere. Suppose the answerer of the question has a history of being blunt.

"Am I fat?"
"No, you're not fat."
Translation: Yes, you might be a little bit fat.

"Am I fat?"
"No, but I suppose you could maybe lose a couple of pounds."
Translation: Yeah, you're definitely fat now.

Consider a third possibility:

"Am I fat?"
"Oh come on, stop fishing for compliments."
Translation: You're absolutely not fat (and you know it!)

Subtext can be delivered through vocal tone, phrasing, delivery, reference to prior experiences, knowledge of relationships, body language, gesticulation, circumstances, and even moods. It can have a lot to do with context, prior history, and the pre-existing relationship. It sounds abstract and confusing, but just imagine that subtext is everything we want to say besides the *exact words* we use.

In fact, that's one of the big reasons we use it. It allows us to navigate the world through indirect and nonconfrontational means. If you're great at subtext, it saves time, it's efficient, and it imparts great emotional intelligence by understanding people's ever-shifting circumstances.

Now, many people will feel that subtext, indirect communication, and nonverbal communication are plain annoying and unnecessary. These might be the kind of people who pride themselves on "telling it like it is" and find the idea of tact, politeness, or social nuances trivial or even entirely optional.

The truth is, however, knowing how to read subtext is an essential social skill. On the surface it may appear illogical and ambiguous, but with practice it can become not only easy to understand, but a valuable tool for successful communication. Learning to read between the lines is a skill that prevents misunderstandings, smooths over potential conflicts, and helps people understand one another better–even if it doesn't seem like it sometimes.

Subtext appears in every situation, from work and dating to social situations and family dynamics. In fact, much of dating can be said to be subtext because most of the sexual tension depends on not revealing true intentions up front. If you ask someone to dinner and they tell you they are busy, they might be busy, or they might not be interested. If you ask the same person out four times and each time they say they're busy, then there is additional subtext for you to read. Take the context into account and things aren't looking good for you on the romantic front.

Through our behavior and choice of words, we transmit clues and desperately hope people pick up on them. Of course, this is the origin of passive-aggressive behavior—we don't feel comfortable saying something directly, so our indirect measures become more and more aggressive and unpleasant. As a species, we are fairly avoidant and nonconfrontational. Not many people feel comfortable wearing their opinions and hearts on their sleeves, especially when they clash with those of other people. Directness is inherently tense, so it's something we prefer to avoid.

A helpful method to imagine how subtext works in social situations is to imagine how it factors into a novel or a screenplay. When you're watching a movie or reading a book, you don't usually get told what the characters understand, feel, or think, and despite that, you come away with a clear sense of meaning about the scenes and relationships. This is all because of subtext.

In this context, it's commonly referred to as what is *under the skin of the character*—what drives and motivates them, what they feel toward everyone else in the story, and what's under the surface of all of their actions. Without giving characters clear motivations and having everyone in the movie operate only on a "what you see is what you get" level, you end up with a flat movie with no emotional impact.

Even in movies, there can be ambiguity in the subtext—sometimes intentional and sometimes not. This is the part the audience must fill in, which is why two people can come out of a film and have radically different ideas about the meaning the director was trying to convey.

Let's take a look at an example scene in detail to illustrate this clearly. Always remember that we have to separate the covert and overt communication.

Imagine a room where a man clasps a tiny baby-blue box in his hands. The table is decorated with roses and Champagne. A woman appears at the side of the frame and prepares to leave the room. She does not notice the man in the corner. He says, "Wait!"

Why does the man call the woman?

If you say, "Because he wants to propose to her," you have understood the subtext present in this basic scene. The dialogue never says that the man wants to propose marriage to the woman. You inferred that from a combination of the mood, the description, and the scene itself.

Is the word "wait" subtext? In this scene, the man is telling the woman to stop. There is nothing hidden in his words other than "Don't go!" or perhaps "Stay!" depending on how the word is delivered.

Imagine instead that the man overtly says, "I have a table laid out here for you and I intend to propose with this beautiful ring I bought from Tiffany & Co." It's not something that would happen in real life, and thus, movies have to be written with subtext that allows people to understand what's happening.

Filling in the details of any incoming communication through subtext is integral to better communication and greater likability. If you look closely, you will soon find that almost everything a person says has shades of subtext meant to consciously or unconsciously communicate additional messages.

Pay attention to people's prior history and experiences and how they might relate to the current situation. What emotions are at play here? Hint: there is always at least one primary emotion at play. It will inevitably color their perspectives, priorities, and motivations in a way that could make their message differ from their words. If you know someone's general personality traits, you can often make a call by analyzing the situation from how they would prefer to conduct themselves. If someone is extremely meek and quiet and says something to the effect of "I agree... I suppose," then it probably means they are internally screaming "NO!" Essentially, consider the source and how a person's experiences color their communication.

Judge someone's authenticity by analyzing the tone of their voice. Are they angry, serious, or sarcastic? Does the tone match the message? If someone says yes but they use a sarcastic tone, then they probably mean no. If someone says yes but they are angry, then they are probably not happy with the outcome. If they are serious and they say yes, then they are conflicted or they probably don't care. There is a virtually unlimited number of interpretations of vocal tone, but most of them indeed mean that the words aren't meant to be taken at face value.

Observe how people respond to you. When you look at how patient people are, how nice they act, and how accommodating they try to be, you can gauge how they feel about what you say. This also extends to how much silence you hear and how much interest they show. If someone takes two beats to answer a simple question, they had to think about their reply and may be using subtext to communicate negativity even if they agree with you.

Another aspect to consider, which may require more intense observational skills, is to see how much they deviate from their usual pattern of behavior. If your supervisor is typically upbeat, what does it mean that they are somber and negative one day? Does your interpretation change if that day is their birthday, or Christmas, or payday? All these tiny details can turn a proclamation of "Things are going well." into the exact opposite message. You can test it out for yourself now: see how many different ways you can say, "Things are going well." Can you see how just a few small tweaks can change the meaning from sincere joy, to doubt, to defensiveness?

Subtext leaves clues that you can harness to become an expert communicator. People leave signs everywhere.

Of course, the tough part is deciphering these aspects of people simultaneously and instantly, as you might do in a normal everyday conversation. This means you actually have two tasks: (1) processing the conversation and responding appropriately and (2) being on the lookout for subtextual cues. You might be able to train yourself to pick up on specific types of subtext and social cues, but can you pick up on them while trying to find others? Or will you only be able to observe so many things at once? It might seem like you'd need three brains and six pairs of eyes to pick up on so many things at once—at the beginning, this might be true.

But the only thing we can do is start small and train yourself until these things become a subconscious habit to consider—*why did they say that, what are they feeling, and what could it mean?*

I want to end the section on subtext with a small exercise to get you into the mood. It's fairly easy: go out into public and observe people interacting—for example, sitting at a café and covertly watching the people at nearby tables. You can't hear the overt conversation, so you're going to make a guess at the subtext of the covert communication. Assign backstories, emotions, and motivations to the people you are observing. Go out on a limb and make up stories. Once you get better at subtext, you'll find that the stories you create in situations like this will become more and more accurate.

What People Laugh at Tells You Who They Are

Most dating profiles mention the importance of a sense of humor, but have you ever considered that humor is as much a personality construct as something like extraversion or creativity?

Psychologist Alberto Dionigi explains that a person's sense of humor is actually a combination of many other aspects of their personality–which makes it especially useful if our goal is to improve our people-reading skills.

Have you ever wondered why you instantly like someone with the same "type" of humor that you have? Have you ever noticed that some people's sense of humor is called "dark" while other people's preferred style of comedy is felt to be more innocent and harmless?

There's a reason for this. Plenty of new research studies now suggest that humor is a potent indicator of our mental habits, coping strategies, strengths, and weaknesses. It can reveal our preferences, values, self-esteem, expectations, mood, identity, cultural background, and even the kind of media we predominantly consume. Rather than humor being somehow outside of the more official personality categories, it may be one of the most central markers of who we are on a core level.

Here are some noteworthy correlations between humor style and personality.

Watch for: self-deprecating humor, or someone who can laugh at their own shortcomings.

"I'd like to kill myself, but I'm afraid of commitment, so I just take a lot of naps."

A little self-deprecating humor can indicate a relatively stable sense of self and psychological resilience. But it's a fine line–if you notice someone consistently mocking themselves or putting themselves down in an attempt to fit in, it could point to a maladaptive coping style. Being a "good sport" is one thing, but if people's self-mockery actually makes others uncomfortable, it could signal genuinely low self-esteem, passive aggression (as a kind of "fishing" behavior), or an attempt to escape or avoid negative feelings.

A single self-deprecating joke likely doesn't mean anything; however, a pattern of consistently making self-defeating jokes may point to more serious issues with depression and anxiety.

Watch for: "dark humor" or finding humor predominantly in satire, cynicism, irony, or sarcasm.

"Huh, tank's empty. Looks like we need to fill it up."
"Oh, you think? Your genius astounds me sometimes."

Consistently dark humor may point to a dark personality. Some research suggests that people high in the "dark triad" trait of Machiavellianism (essentially, being manipulative) tend to laugh at humor that has a nasty edge of cruelty or mockery (Dionigi et. al., 2022).

For some people, such humor may even be a way for them to control others, for example, invalidating, attacking, or demeaning someone while claiming "it's just a joke!" or using jokes to embarrass others. If someone is in the habit of laughing at the concept of manipulation itself, it may suggest a comfort and familiarity with the use of manipulation in their own lives.

Watch for: humor that elevates the joke-maker's status-or lowers everyone else's.

"You know, I always feel more intelligent after reading your work."

Not all dark personality traits are associated with dark humor types. Dionigi explains that narcissists and psychopaths may in fact favor "lighter" humor types (fun, silliness, nonsense, wit) but use them in a toxic way.

Pay attention to whether someone uses humor to indirectly lower the status of someone else, elevate their own status, or both. This may reflect a more general tendency towards antisocial behavior or a lack of empathy.

You may need to pay very close attention to the way narcissists in particular use humor; they may be incredibly fun and charming people, but the intended result is always to consolidate their own superior status in the eyes of others. Look for consistent patterns of attention-seeking, grandiose storytelling, and a certain theatricality to jokes.

A good example of status-based or narcissistic joke-telling is someone who makes a joke they know the other person won't understand, in an attempt to appear more intelligent. Another example is a sly, backhanded compliment made just for the pleasure of watching the other person try to figure out whether they've been insulted or not. Yet another example is "pranksters" who seem unconcerned that nobody is enjoying their antics. Finally, notice if someone likes to hog the "limelight" or gets competitive about who gets to be the "funny one" in social situations.

Watch for: laughing at violence.

Most of us tend to find the mild misfortune of others amusing–this is pie-in-the-face or slipping-on-banana-peel territory. However, pay close attention if a person finds outright violence entertaining. Laughing at gratuitous gore or real crime may show extreme moral disengagement or a degree of desensitization (Allen et. al., 2022, *Who finds media violence funny? Testing the effects of media violence exposure and dark personality traits*). Essentially, you are witnessing a person who is capable of "turning off" their morality, empathy, and sense of justice. Someone to steer clear of!

Watch for: humor that favors witty jokes and "banter" between friends.

"Hey losers!"
"Hey! Welcome, you look like you'll fit right in. Want to be our chairman?"
"Well, someone has to keep up the standard around here."

"Standards!? That's against club rules and you know it."

"Wait, we have standards AND rules? When did all this happen?"

"Well, something had to be done after that shirt Ben wore last week."

"Yeah, sorry Ben, we didn't want to say but the lady next door reported you to the police. Hope you don't mind, but we said we didn't know you."

Not everyone shares the same sense of humor, and not everyone is going to find the same things funny. However, it's worth taking note of the *function* of humor, rather than just its content. You've probably noticed how a woman on a date with a guy she likes will tend to laugh at his jokes–whether they're funny or not. Why? The function of both the jokes he makes and her laughter is clear: to signal interest, to strengthen their bond, and to communicate mutual interest.

The same can be said for any kind of pro-social banter that is made not exactly because it's funny, but because its unspoken intention is to make everyone feel good. Witty chat amongst friends (the Irish have their own word for it: craic) may actually lower everyone's anxiety and depression, and strengthen feelings of group cohesion. A person who responds well to this sort of humor is sending a clear message:

they value social connection and are willing to make efforts to behave pro-socially.

Watch for: humor made in the face of adversity.

"What! You have cancer?!"
"Shh, keep your voice down or everyone else will want it, too!"

A person who responds to tragedy, awkwardness, or discomfort with humor is demonstrating their own resilience and giving you a glimpse into their style of coping. Of course, it's a matter of degree: someone who seemingly can never be serious about anything may be revealing a tendency to avoid unpleasant feelings or else overcompensate for them. Be curious about why they may be doing this, and the broader role this kind of "humor" is playing for them.

Often, people laugh to relieve the tension of a situation, and the things they find most outrageous and funny are actually the things they are most anxious and unsettled about within themselves. If you observe what people tend to find most ridiculous and hilarious in others, you may see a reflection of their own inverted values. For instance, consistently laughing at people who mispronounce words or make social faux pas may point to an anxiety around one's own intelligence or social standing.

Watch closely for the person who always seems to know how to defuse tension or resolve conflicts with a well-timed joke. They are demonstrating enormous empathy and social sophistication. This is likely someone who is mature, self-aware, and capable of self-reflection.

Humor is, of course, a very subjective phenomenon, but we can learn a lot about someone by simply noticing what they laugh at. You can also observe the reverse of all the above points, for example if someone flat-out refuses to laugh at violence in a movie, they may be demonstrating a robust moral sense. Similarly, someone who consistently dismisses or ignores friendly group banter is sending a clear message: "I'm not interested in affiliation. I don't consider myself part of this group."

Takeaways:

- We've talked about values and rational intentions that people might have. This chapter focuses on emotional cues that we can use to analyze people, and taken together, we are able to better predict and understand both rational and emotional states.

- Better understanding people's emotions begins with understanding your own. This comes in the form of emotional intelligence, and Daniel Goleman's conception of emotional intelligence consists of self-awareness (what do I feel and why), self-management (how can I express my emotions safely and learn from them), self-motivation (what makes me happy, and how can I achieve that), and social awareness (what are other people feeling and why. The whole process begins with understanding yourself and then realizing that everyone else has the same amount of unconscious and hidden thoughts that dictate their emotions and actions. It is a way of thinking that must be trained and allows you to pull a significant amount of information from a small interaction.
- Likewise, we must learn to understand subtextual cues better. This is related to the social awareness element of emotional intelligence. We must realize that most communication is covert, and yet most of us are only responding to communication that is overt. This means we frequently miss the true meaning of people's words and actions. The easiest way to adopt this particular method of thinking is to ask, *why did they say that, what are they feeling, and what could it mean?*
- You can learn a lot about people by

observing the things they laugh at. Finding violence, cynicism, sarcasm, and manipulation funny can signal dark personality traits, whereas good natured, witty, and pro-social banter serves a completely different function, and may correlate with better psychological health and resilience.

Chapter 5. Just Ask

Famous Greek philosopher Aristotle once stated, "Knowing yourself is the beginning of all wisdom," and founding father of the United States of America Benjamin Franklin seemed to espouse similar thoughts: "There are three things extremely hard: steel, a diamond, and to know oneself." One is saying that self-awareness is the root of wisdom, while the other is saying that self-awareness is a difficult state to achieve.

Of course, this book is not necessarily about self-awareness; however, we know that the process of gaining self-awareness is both a pre-condition and an inevitable result of learning to read and analyze people better. In a sense, it's something that is simple–but not especially easy.

As you read through the previous chapters, you may have wondered to yourself, "Jeez, all this subterfuge and guesswork–why not just *ask* people the things you want to know?" And that's a very good question! The scientists among us will already know that in many ways, you cannot really observe a phenomenon if you are yourself part of the phenomenon. Socially speaking, the moment you ask someone a question, you are in some sense changing what they are.

Consider that people are always motivated to present their own version of themselves to the world, for their own reasons. This agenda may be nothing more than wanting to appear in as flattering a light as possible, but it could extend to outright concealment, deception, and deceit. Analyzing people *without them being aware* that you are analyzing them is a way to observe them underneath that mask. It almost always gives a more accurate "reading."

That said, you can indeed learn a lot about people by noticing the mask they deliberately choose to wear (why, for example, did they choose that mask and not some other mask?) and you can glean a lot about people's values, goals and assumptions by looking at what they choose to present... and what they choose to ignore or conceal. This is an art in itself, but not the focus of this current chapter. Instead, we will be focusing here on what we can discover about others through *indirect* questions. From there, we can learn much about people based on their answers. In many ways, it mirrors what we can understand about ourselves through the same process.

How do people typically gain self-awareness? The focus is geared around people asking themselves simple and direct questions that hopefully hint at realizations just outside our conscious knowledge. Typically, they'll ask themselves questions, such as "What makes me happy and fulfilled?" Such direct questions should be considered a mediocre starting point, because these questions force you to ramble and create an answer out of nothing. In *deliberately* generating a response, you lose any genuine expression and the truth seems to somehow evaporate. It often doesn't lead to much insight other than pretty platitudes. You might lie or even interpret the question in unhelpful ways.

Seriously, try to answer that previous question right now in a way that actually gives you some meaning and direction. Can you do it?

If not, or if you find yourself babbling on about the things you think you *should* say in response to such a question, then you may be beginning to understand one of the weaknesses of asking others the same kind of question. Really, unless the question is, "What's your name?", there is often very little that's "direct" in a direct question!

What about if you were asked something like, "What parts of your week do you look forward to the most" or "What would you do if you won the lottery and could choose how to spend your time?" or "What is your favorite type of long-term vacation?"

Try answering these questions. They likely elicit more concrete answers—specific pieces of you or other people—that you can work with and seek to delve into. Suddenly, you seem like a more real, more three-dimensional person. When it comes to indirect questions, we are asking about people's behaviors, which form a more accessible and obvious source of information. Answers to these "simple" questions can actually provide the most complex and rich insights, and provide the best basis for understanding people on a deeper level. Thoughts and intentions are important, but ultimately, if they are never translated into action, they are largely useless for our purposes.

If you consider your own responses to the questions above, you can see how much easier it is to interpret and extrapolate the larger, more abstract themes. You may *say*, for example, that it's your family that makes you feel most happy and fulfilled, but if your favorite type of vacation is a solo trip, if you find yourself looking forward to Mondays, and if you remember your colleague's birthdays more readily than your children's, then a truer, more nuanced picture of the person you really are starts to emerge...

Indirect Questions; Direct Information

This chapter provides a novel way to analyze people. Through innocent questioning, we can uncover a host of information that represents an entire worldview or set of values. For instance, what if you were to ask someone where they obtained their news and which television channel, which set of publications, which magazines, and which pundits or hosts they preferred? It's a prime illustration of an indirect question that lets you understand quite a bit about how they think. It involves a bit of extrapolation and guesswork, but at least there's a concrete piece of information to go on and many concrete associations with it. Furthermore, most people are unguarded about this kind of information and will happily volunteer it without a second thought.

We start this chapter with some of these indirect questions before going even more in-depth by asking people for stories and seeing what we can glean from those. These questions are phrased to challenge and inspire deep thought. They ask people to dive deeper such that we can begin to understand their behavioral and thought patterns. They're the kind of questions that will yield interesting insights, but don't feel intrusive in the slightest.

1. What kind of prize would you work hardest for, and what punishment would you work hardest to avoid?

The answer to this question might help identify the true motive behind an individual's drive. Beyond surface-level things, what is really motivating people? What do they really care about? And what type of pain or pleasure matters to them? On an instinctual level, what really matters the most in both a positive and negative way? In a way, this answer also reflects values.

For example, gamblers all want one prize: the jackpot. They try and try again, whether it be with scratchers or slot machines to try and win the big prize money. Are they motivated by winning back their losses? Is their hope to become richer than they can imagine? Do they actually want it, or are they filling a void and keeping themselves distracted?

Why are they working so hard? You might surmise that their motivation is the thrill and rush of the risk involved. Do they care about making steady pay or finding their purpose? Maybe, and maybe not. When you can dig into what someone wants the most and why, you can often find what is driving them without having to ask it directly. The way people answer this question will clearly tell you their priorities and what they consider pain and pleasure in their lives.

Look for the emotion behind people's answers here, and you can get a pretty good read on their values. A goal of rising to CEO-level doesn't just exist in a vacuum—what are the feelings, emotions, and fulfilled expectations that come from wanting it? Likewise, wanting to avoid being poor speaks to very specific desires for security and safety from danger.

2. Where do you want to spend money, and where do you accept skimping on or skipping altogether?

This answer reveals what matters to someone's life and what they want to experience or avoid. This is not really about the item or items to be purchased; there comes a point where material belongings no longer have a use, and it's about what those items represent and provide. For example, sometimes, spending money on experiences instead of a new purse has the potential to improve someone's overall well-being and outlook on life. Again, look for the underlying emotions and motivations behind the answer.

So what do you have no problem splurging on, and what doesn't matter to you? For instance, when deciding on vacation expenditures, people may opt to splurge on an epic boat excursion and stay in a shabby hotel. This reveals their desire to experience an unforgettable moment rather than staying in a nice hotel with golden toilets, which they view as a waste of money. Others might opt for the opposite and revel in their creature comforts while not seeing much of the scenery. In either case, they've used their money to quite literally identify and spend toward their priorities and values.

Where your money goes is an important part of what makes you happy, so if you can pay attention to where you let it flow and where you cut it off, you'll immediately know what matters to you on a daily basis. Contrast this question to if you were to ask someone, "What do you value in your daily life?" Again, there is a concrete answer here to analyze.

This same principle applies equally to time, money, and effort. Where these things flow, whether consciously or unconsciously, represents the values people possess.

3. What is your most personally significant and meaningful achievement and also your most meaningful disappointment or failure?

It's common that experiences, whether they're good or bad, shape people into who they are. Achievements and failures tie into how someone sees oneself. Significant experiences also tend to create their self-identities—*you are this kind of person because you did this and succeeded or failed*. We can't escape the fact that past occurrences will often influence our current and future actions. They don't have to, but this isn't a book about changing your mindsets. The point is that large events will reverberate throughout our entire lives.

So this question will get a response about how people view themselves, for better or worse. Failure will painfully poke perceived flaws they hate about themselves, while achievements will bring up the strengths they are proud of.

A career woman who has worked her way up the corporate ladder might proudly reflect on her accomplishment. Why does she consider this her greatest achievement? Because she values independence, resilience, and determination, and that's exactly what it takes to get to that career pinnacle. She looks back to the things she did in order to get that corner office, and she feels positively about them.

Thus, the answer about her career accomplishments is actually a story about the positive traits she utilized in reaching that point—her self-identity. You can imagine that the same negative type of self-identity might unfold if the same woman were to talk about her failures and ended up in a job that she despised. Those are the exact things she hates the most.

The way that people answer this question shows who they want to be, and this is reflected in exactly how their expectations have either been fulfilled or not.

4. What is effortless and what is always exhausting?

This is a question that is designed to better understand what people actually enjoy. Something that is effortless isn't always an innate talent, but rather an indication that they enjoy it. On the other hand, something that is always exhausting is not always about people's lack of competency, but rather a distaste for the actual activity. Thus, answers to this question can indicate where people find natural joy and enjoyment, even if they don't realize it themselves.

For instance, as a baker answers this question, she may recognize her rather mediocre capacity for creativity for blending ingredients together to make a dessert. Although she is above average, she is not naturally talented at it, and it has been very difficult for as long as she can remember. She was not innately talented with culinary creativity, and yet she finds joy in it such that she is always driven to it. It's challenging but effortless in a way that she doesn't grow tired of.

On the other hand, she may have a natural talent in understanding and following traditional recipes—yet it is not something that she values or particularly cares about. If we were to look at only her innate talents, we would conclude that she should stick to only executing the dishes of others. But it's simply not what she values. As mentioned previously, wherever our time, effort, energy, and money goes, such are our values.

5. If you could design a character in a game, what traits would you emphasize and which would you ignore?

This question asks what people see as their ideal self and also what they feel is less important in the world. Imagine that you have a limited number of points to give a person but six traits to spread the points across. Which will you choose to emphasize and bolster, and which will you choose to leave average or even lacking?

Suppose you have the ability to choose between the traits of charisma, academic intelligence, sense of humor, honesty, resilience, and emotional awareness. The traits you'd choose to put the maximum number of points in is how you'd like others to see you. It may represent your current composition of traits, or it might be completely opposite to who you currently are. In either case, it's more than likely that this either represents how you see yourself or how you would like to see yourself. And the other traits? Well, they simply matter less. In turn, they seek out people with those traits they like and are less keen to seek out those with the other traits. There are probably stories behind each of the traits that people might choose as well.

A related question to ask others is, "What traits are common in other people?" This question comes from a 2010 psychological study by Dustin Wood, in which he found that people tended to describe others with similar traits as themselves. Presumably this is because people tend to see their own qualities in others. No one believes that their mental makeup of traits is uncommon, and thus, they believe everyone has a similar perspective and way of thinking to them. Answers to this question are a direct insight into what traits people believe they have, for better or worse. From there, you know what kind of approach they have to the world—kind, generous, distrusting, mischievous, or even ill-spirited.

6. What charity would you donate millions to if you had to?

Answering this question forces one to answer what they care about in the world at large rather than just in their own life.

Will you donate to an animal shelter or a charity for cancer? Perhaps you would sponsor a child from a third-world country? They all say very different things. You might have had a first- or secondhand experience with any of these causes. Whatever the case, it shows what matters when people start to think outside of themselves. You can see a whole sector of the world that they are concerned about, and this allows you to see how they view their place in the world. In other words, whose interests do they tend to prioritize or be motivated by? As always, look to the underlying emotion.

Being able to ask these questions evokes a deeper connection to people's values, ideas, and awareness. The purpose of asking these is to, again, examine behavior. These questions guide a person in thinking about the most relevant aspects of his or her character. They also make people think beyond predictable statements and organically stimulate more meaningful thought. Look beyond the answers and read between the lines. Critical thinking, evaluation, and reflection are the key skills at play here.

Next, we go deeper by asking people for stories that they construct, rather than just a relatively short answer, to see what we can glean from hearing their internal dialogue in full effect.

Stories and the Inner Dialogue

The more you are able to hear people talk about their inner thoughts and desires, the more information you have to make guesses and analyses. As with before, getting indirect stories is going to be more effective than directly asking for someone's life story.

The overall goal here is to draw meaning from people's subconscious thought. When you ask yourself a pointed question (such as "What makes me happy?"), you likely aren't going to be able to answer that question. Even if you do answer the question, it probably won't be an answer that helps you achieve greater happiness.

So what stories do others tell themselves, and what can we learn from them?

There are two primary methods of interest: Kate Wendleton's seven stories exercise and a personality test from psychologist Carl Jung. Both seek to evaluate personality based on answers that people give to seemingly unrelated questions. Indeed, in a moment, you'll understand why they can be seen like either a horoscope or an illuminating look into someone's psyche, depending on who you're talking to.

The Seven Stories Exercise

Kate Wendleton, career counselor, created this exercise out of Bernard Haldane's work in helping military personnel transition into civilian work.

After World War II in the 1940s, the job market began to get flooded with veterans returning home and looking for work. It was very evident that many businesses and organizations didn't possess the resources or skills to capitalize on these veterans' talents and capacities. Veterans were accustomed to jobs that pertained to war. These jobs weren't necessarily available or well-known in the general labor force. They simply had no idea how to evaluate them. Sounds similar to the MBTI, doesn't it?

Haldane wanted to do something to help the veterans. First, he asked veterans to recollect their best achievements while at the same time clarifying what they enjoyed doing the most. Next, he helped them clarify their individual strengths and skills that were transferable. Specifically, the focus was to identify ones that could be useful to an employer.

Third, Haldane helped them market and present their offerings in a way that appealed to a potential employer. He would help the employer recognize the benefits of hiring veterans based on their skills, achievements, and enjoyments.

Traditional methods for finding jobs always used an outside-in approach. In other words, old methods would try to fit people into jobs, rather than fitting people's skills to jobs. Although it was deemed to be extremely radical at the time, Haldane's inside-out approach was able to help many veterans who needed assistance in seeking employment.

The seven stories ask people to complete the following steps.

Step One: Write Down 25 Accomplishments

People were asked to identify 25 accomplishments that they felt especially good about. This would involve having people reflect on life accomplishments that ranged from childhood all the way to adulthood. The answers should be specific and not just a general statement. Normally, people may have a hard time with this, but they should really just go with their gut. They should write down whatever makes them feel good. Twenty-five is a lot of *anything* to think about, but the point is that you dig deep and leave no stone unturned. It could be a rather insignificant accomplishment, but the underlying feeling of triumph could be massive and educational.

For instance, someone might write that they were elected class president during their sophomore year in high school or that they coordinated a charity fundraiser selling car wash tickets to benefit the homeless while in their junior year of college. In the grand scheme of life, these are irrelevant, but they speak to particular traits and values.

Step Two: Narrow Down to Seven Accomplishments

From the list of 25, people should now narrow their list down to the seven most important and significant ones that have made them happy. At this point, it will probably become clear that people will choose personal significance over actual magnitude of achievement. That's what this process is all about.

They may select achievements such as overcoming cancer when they were 32 years old by actively going to treatment and changing their entire lifestyles. They might also recall putting together their first furniture all on their own when first moving into their house. Again, it can even be something as small as speaking in public and not breaking down. There is no definition or criteria for which seven you should use. Chances are you'll be able to figure out which are the most significant to you.

Step Three: Write Stories Associated with Those Seven Accomplishments

Taking from the seven narrowed accomplishments, people are to write out the stories that were associated with each of them. From here, they should be able to identify the skills and lessons learned and manifested from those experiences. Identify what exactly made them so personally significant. Write the story in the first or third person and make sure to include the context and the aftermath of how you felt afterward.

When people are able to go through their experiences, they may be able to identify the elements of those experiences and how those elements made them happy. They can see commonalities in those experiences as well as certain aspects that attributed to their happiness. Write out the emotions felt in as much detail as possible and attempt to reflect in the story why there were such feelings of triumph and happiness.

Those who overcame cancer might talk about how they became much more optimistic in their outlooks on life as well as more resilient when faced with adversity. They remember those agonizing moments of chemotherapy but the great ways that the nursing staff helped them throughout the process. They saw the compassion that medical staff had for patients and, in turn, became more positive and uplifted.

For the people who put together furniture for the first time, they might recall feeling independent and able to follow directions once they really focused their attention to it. They remembered what it felt like to read through instructions that seemed like another language at first. They would also remember that great feeling of tightening that last screw and placing the furniture in the perfect spot in the house. It might sound trivial, but remember, it's about the feelings and emotions it gave you, not about the achievement itself.

Step Four: Analyze Those Stories

In a deeper purpose, people would now reflect and analyze what they learned from their experiences. Moreover, people can look back on all of their older experiences and attempt to connect them to ones pertaining to the seven stories.

Besides the cancer survivors learning about their feelings after the experience, they are now able to analyze their overall feeling of the process. They might discover that all of the experiences, even when negative, happened for a reason and they were meant to prosper through it all. They reminisce about all the things they used to love to do, like playing soccer or drawing, prior to being diagnosed with their condition. As a result, it motivates them to overcome this ailment and work toward participating in those hobbies again.

The homeowners may learn overall that they truly enjoy the beauty and struggles of homeownership. They start with a piece of furniture and then can feel confident about moving on to bigger home projects like tile and floor replacements. They start to walk around the house and notice that the bathroom could get a little bit of a facelift. This motivation to do more because they loved the sense of accomplishment helps them power through their initial fear of not being a "do-it-yourselfer."

The idea behind the seven stories is to be able to triangulate what people truly value and want, in their own words.

Carl Jung Personality Test

Another popular test used to evaluate personality comes from Carl Jung. Carl Jung was abnormally analytical in his thinking. He drew a lot of influence from Buddhist ways of thinking, which then translated to the way he viewed and studied people and their personalities. He believed that there was a deeper connection to the way that people thought about simple things.

Although simple things are easier to identify, it's the answers that people provided that would reveal more about the person they were and how they preferred to do things. From how they view other people to how they envision their deaths, the questions from his personality test were very unique and intriguing. It's always been attributed to Carl Jung, but it seems to have gained a lot of popularity from the book *Diary* by Chuck Palahniuk. Take this test a bit more tongue in cheek than the rest of the book.

The test asks individuals to answer the following.

First, name a color. Any color. Now think of three descriptive adjectives that describe that color.

Second, name an animal. Any animal. Now think of three descriptive adjectives that describe that animal.

Third, name a body of water. Name three descriptive adjectives describing it.

Fourth, imagine you're in a room. All the walls are white and there are no windows or doors. Describe in three descriptive adjectives how that room feels to you.

Stop here. Complete the questions. Then read on to see what they could mean about you. The basis behind each question is where the evaluation and analysis really happen.

Question one: (color choice) the three words represent how you see yourself.
Question two: (animal choice) the three words represent how you see other people.
Question three: (body of water choice) the three words represent your preferred sex life.
The last question: (white room description) the three words represent your death.

Let's take a look at what each question and answer might be revealing. To reiterate, the answers you gave are not the important part; the adjectives you used are.

For instance, someone answers the following:
Teal: happy, cool, calming
Deer: timid, quiet, scared
Waterfall: raging, powerful, strong
White room: calm, tranquil, confusing

According to the test, this person sees themselves as happy, cool, and calming. Meanwhile, they see others as timid, quiet, and scared around them. They view sex as raging, powerful, and strong, and when they think of death, they think of calm, tranquility, and confusion.

Each of these questions has an interesting way of describing people based on the answers they provide. Although people believe they are just answering normal and easy questions, they are providing a deeper indication into who they are as a person. It's probably less scientific than anything else in this book, but it does provide food for thought and, at worst, is a great game to play with a date. It's more similar to a free-association word game or a Rorschach test a psychologist might administer. Whatever is on your mind exists for a reason, and constructing these answers and stories merely gives you an excuse to identify them.

These stories, taken with the questions from earlier in this chapter, are merely methods of bringing out people's true intentions.

Catching Deception Through 3 Easy Questions

Let's conclude our chapter on a more controversial topic: lies. There are plenty of old wives' tales on how best to spot a lie, as well as mountains of advice from the so-called experts who are happy to share their foolproof methods. The truth of lie-detection, however, is far less encouraging: on the whole, it's a pretty difficult thing to do. Ironically, the people who claim to be in the possession of the "one easy trick" are often just... lying.

The fact is that human beings are either quite good at lying, or quite bad at detecting lies, or perhaps a bit of both. That said, the research in this area does suggest that accuracy *can* be improved if clusters of behavior are interpreted against baseline, rather than analysing isolated things like scratching your nose or using this or that telling phrase.

One major principle in lie-detection is this: in order to know what a lie looks like, we need to know what the truth looks like. This allows us to make meaningful comparisons. It also means that detecting falsehoods in strangers (or people who have lied to you consistently) is almost impossible.

According to Jack Schafer, skilled ex-FBI agent and author of the 2015 bestseller, *The Like Switch: An Ex-FBI Agent's Guide to Influencing, Attracting, and Winning People Over*, there are predictable patterns in the ways that liars express themselves. Let's recap some of his lie-detecting advice:

Tip1: Look out for feigned memory loss, for example, clearly pretending not to recall something that otherwise would be very easy to recall. "Oh, I don't remember." is often just a way of trying to squirm out of lying outright.

Tip 2: Listen for passive language, i.e., grammatical constructions that sneakily remove the subject/actor of the sentence. For example, saying, "the watch was stolen" is a way of concealing the person responsible for stealing it. When someone consistently uses the passive voice even when it's awkward or unnatural, they may be trying to pull your attention away from the guilty subject.!

Other grammatical tell-tales are when people go to lengths to explain what they *didn't* do, rather than what they *did*. Liars also tend to stick a little too much to the facts, and leave out their emotions; truth tellers will relay their feelings and opinions as part of their story, sometimes including their own reactions and interpretations as part of their remembered experience, "I walked in that morning, and I saw the watch was gone, and I remember thinking it was strange…"

Tip 3: Take note of "protesting too much." Someone who is telling a lie might labor the point a little too forcefully, and end up supplying far too much unnecessary detail and justification. If it sounds like they're spent a lot of time carefully rehearsing a long story with all sorts of complicated details, consider the possibility that they have in fact rehearsed it and have already told themselves this story in anticipation of the lie.

Conversely, people who have actually experienced an event may take a little longer to express it neatly in words, and they may actually supply fewer details and justifications. They may tell a tale that is more unstructured. Truthful stories often include more sensory data, dialogue, and emotions, and may focus on unexpected events, rather than emphasize the normality of everything.

Liars will often present overly factual and detailed information, such as precise times and dates–something that truthtellers don't do as often. When asked about their story, truthtellers tend to simply repeat it again and again, without changing much, whereas a liar will keep adding more information and justifications the more they are interrogated.

In the same vein, pay attention to people who respond to a question with another question, or those who answer a question that you didn't actually ask. Be especially cognizant of people who avoid a question entirely, especially if it's to shift blame.

Tip 4: Notice if they include mistakes. Truthtellers have no problem correcting something shown to be a mistake, and they have no problem recounting a story that makes them look a little bad. A liar, however, is far less likely to self-correct, and are much less motivated to construct a false story that is embarrassing or stupid sounding (they may be more ready to paint others in a denigrating light, however). They do not want to appear to be unsure of what they're saying, and so may cling to a story even when a truthteller would happily admit they've made a small error.

Here's a neat trick: deliberately introduce an error yourself in the story they're supplying, and relay that error back to them, then watch to see if they correct you. A liar is far more likely to let the mistake slip (it doesn't matter to them, right?), whereas a truth teller will correct you.

Tip 5: Watch for increased cognitive load. Basically, lying is hard work. It requires more processing power from your brain than simply recalling a true event. For that reason, you can sometimes detect falsehoods in that people seem to take that little bit longer to relay information to you.

They may stall for time, ask for questions to be repeated, or waffle in a slightly too formal tone, as though they were in a court of law or extra careful of saying the wrong thing. The cognitive lag is often because the person is literally trying to keep up with their own lie, or else make something up in the moment. Overall, there may be a feeling of things not quite adding up, or, paradoxically, of everything being just a little too neat and perfect. There may be a subtle mismatch felt between the details and their emotion while relaying the details, for example describing how upset they were but in a bored, detached way.Pay attention, as always, to your gut feelings.

As you can see, however, all these tips can still leave you with a pretty high failure rate. Another, possibly more useful technique is using strategic questions designed to reveal deception. A research paper was published in the Journal of Forensic Accounting Research (yes, there is such a thing!) titled *A preliminary examination of the effectiveness of assessment questions in detecting dishonest behavior* (Jensen & Smith, 2021). In it, the authors suggest three highly practical and easy-to-ask questions that can help uncover a deception.

These indirect questions have been inspired by the work of criminal investigators and others who make their living from skilful interrogation. Bear in mind that these questions are intended for situations where there has been a rather serious breach of trust and suspected deception, such as a workplace incident or violation like theft or other misconduct in a social setting. It goes without saying that serious crimes require the intervention of the law!

Question 1: "What do you think should happen to the person who's responsible for this crime/offense/action?"

Let's say someone has taken hundreds of dollars from the church petty cash tin in the office. The culprit is at large and it's an unsolved mystery. However, people talk, and everyone has their opinions. Listen closely to these opinions, and try to ask the above question.

Truthtellers tend to want rather harsh punishments for the crime. After all, they haven't done it, and they don't identify with the criminal in any way, so they are more comfortable with recommending the perpetrator experience the full consequences. They are not in a defensive position, nor are they rationalizing their behavior in any way.

Someone who is guilty but trying to hide it, however, will unconsciously feel the need to protect themselves, and cannot help but suggest lighter punishments. They may subtly downplay the crime, or show a little sympathy and leniency for the wrongdoer. They may offer a rationalization that seems out of place. Also be on the lookout for someone very keen to just write off the incident and move on. "Oh well, I guess we'll never know." Truthtellers tend to want to know!

Question 2: "Who do you think has had the opportunity to commit this crime/offense/action?"

By asking people to consider the motivations of others in their group or organization, you are asking them to demonstrate to you their own thought processes on the matter. Guilty individuals tend to name people, departments, or groups that are actually quite unlikely to be responsible–it's as though they're merely pulling names from the air. In fact, this is pretty much what they're doing; by widening the pool of suspects they hope to muddy the waters and hide themselves more effectively.

However, innocent people who are genuinely concerned with finding out the truth tend not to want to randomly accuse anyone and everyone. A liar might say, "Well, *anyone* could have done it–even the Vicar's six-month old daughter could have done it, since I've seen her near the office once or twice." A truthteller, however, might give a more thoughtful and logical response, "Well, it could have been Janet, since she has a key to the office. But the money went missing on a Saturday, and I know the cleaning staff come in on a Saturday, so maybe it could have been them?"

Question 3: "How common do you think this crime/offense/action really is?"

This can be a very revealing question, as people who are trying to deceive will seldom be careful when giving an answer to it. A truthful person will think that the crime is rare. In a sense, for them, it *is* rare–after all, this may be the first time they're even hearing of it, so the event in question seems unusual and unexpected to them. They might say, "Oh, not common at all!" or "I don't ever remember this kind of thing happening before." They will treat the occurrence as unusual, unexpected, and regrettable.

A liar, on the other hand, will be more psychologically familiar with the event, having just committed it, and this cannot help but distort their appraisal. They may also unconsciously try to make the behavior seem more normal and expected than it is, again in order to downplay their own culpability. They may be far more willing to display a casual and accepting stance to the crime. "Theft in churches? Well, sadly, I think it happens all the time these days. Times are tough, after all."

It's worth repeating once more that these questions, though powerful, are not 100% foolproof. Remember that individual people have their own idiosyncratic responses to being questioned, and it can be tricky to distinguish nonverbal signals of guilt from the ordinary stress responses people demonstrate when they know they're under suspicion. Keep your wits about you, don't give too much away, and gather as much information as you can. Detecting lies is difficult, but in time you may gather just enough data to help you find out what you need to know.

Takeaways:

- The traits of analyzing others and self-awareness are inseparable. Knowledge in one realm begets knowledge in the other. This chapter focuses on the ways we can gain valuable information from others by simply asking. Notably, these questions are somewhat indirect and also about behaviors and actions, not intentions or thoughts. Thoughts are too easily corrupted or otherwise simply not representative of what you actually feel. When you can learn about behaviors and actions, you can work from concrete information and analyze with a basis in something real.
- Sometimes the best way to discover something about ourselves is to ask seemingly innocent questions, then read between the lines. The way we answer these types of questions can be more honest and indicative than intentionally trying to figure out your personality and identity. This also begins our process of learning how to analyze information we gain from others and dig below the surface and find possible explanations.
- Besides some specific questions that force people to answer about their values in other terms, we can solicit information through a couple of types of stories. After all, the more we hear someone's internal dialogue, the more insight we can gain. The first way to do this is through the seven stories exercise,

which implores you to ask about people's seven greatest accomplishments and write the stories involved in those triumphs. What comes out in the story will tell you more about who they are and what they value.

- The second method to discover yourself is through Carl Jung's personality test, which consists of four questions: name a color, name an animal, name a body of water, and think about a white room. The ensuing adjectives people use to describe each of those answers may tell you something specific about their personality that may not be conscious.

- When used skillfully, assessment questions can help detect deception. Though catching a lie is much harder than it looks, you can gather interesting data by asking the potential deceiver about their opinions on punishment/consequences, who they think may have done it, and how common the incident is in their estimation. Their answers can be revealing.

Chapter 6. The Motivation Factor

We've tried to identify people's emotional state, as well as what their conscious values are. These two aspects alone can cover the bulk of the work of analyzing who somebody is. However, a more significant underpinning factor of both emotions and values is the motivation that they draw from them. In other words, *why* do people behave as they do?

All of this simply comes down to understanding the way people think and behave by understanding the values that cause them to think and behave that way. It's a question of cause and effect. Most human beings want only a handful of things, although we might all differ a little in how we rank and weight these different needs, and we certainly differ in how we believe we can best go about meeting those needs.

If you can zoom in and really grasp a person's true motivations, you can understand them so much better, perhaps even to the point of being able to predict how they might act in the future. Using this psychological approach gives you the opportunity to get into the perspective of other people, finding clarity on exactly what they *gain* by thinking and behaving as they do. With this knowledge, your interactions with people are instantly enriched.

Again, these intertwine neatly with emotions and values because they are often seeking the same ends. It's just another perspective on why someone will act in the way they do and what we can understand of them from that. We can understand it this way: an individual's essence and personality is a coherent whole, but we can take different perspectives on that whole by asking different questions. Asking *what* someone values yields different data on the same phenomenon as asking *why* they value it, or indeed *how* they value it. Let's look closer.

Pleasure or Pain

Out of all the speculations about the sources of motivation, none is more famous than the *pleasure principle*. The reason it's so renowned is because it's also the easiest to understand.

The pleasure principle was first raised in public consciousness by the father of psychoanalysis, Sigmund Freud, though researchers as far back as Aristotle in ancient Greece noted how easily we could be manipulated and motivated by pleasure and pain.

The pleasure principle asserts that the human mind does everything it can to seek out pleasure and avoid pain. It doesn't get simpler than that. This is the operating system of an amoeba–go towards what feels good, move away from what feels bad. In that simplicity, we find some of life's most universal and predictable motivators.

The pleasure principle is employed by our reptile brain, which can be said to house our natural drives and desires. It doesn't have any sense of restraint. It is primal and unfiltered. It goes after whatever it can to meet our body's urges for happiness and fulfillment. Anything that causes pleasure is felt by the brain the same way, whether it's a tasty meal or a drug. An apt comparison, in fact, is a drug addict who will stop at nothing to get another taste of narcotics.

There are a few rules that govern the pleasure principle, which also make us fairly predictable.

Every decision we make is based on gaining pleasure or avoiding pain. This is the common motivation for every person on earth. No matter what we do in the course of our day, it all gets down to the pleasure principle. You raid the refrigerator for snacks because you crave the taste and feel of certain food. You get a haircut because you think it will make you more attractive to someone else, which will make you happy, which is pleasure.

Conversely, you wear a protective mask while you're using a blowtorch because you want to avoid sparks flying into your face and eyes, because that will be painful. If you trace all of our decisions back, whether short-term or long-term, you'll find that they all stem from a small set of pleasures or pains.

People work harder to avoid pain than to get pleasure. While everyone wants pleasure as much as they can get it, their motivation to avoid pain is actually far stronger. The instinct to survive a threatening situation is more immediate than eating your favorite candy bar, for instance. So when faced with the prospect of pain, the brain will work harder than it would to gain access to pleasure.

For example, imagine you're standing in the middle of a desert road. In front of you is a treasure chest filled with money and outlandishly expensive jewelry that could set you up financially for the rest of your life. But there's also an out-of-control semi careening toward it. You're probably going to make the decision to jump away from the truck rather than grab the treasure chest, because your instinct to avoid pain—in this case, certain death—outweighed your desire to gain pleasure.

If you've hit rock bottom and faced a massive amount of pain or displeasure, then you simply must start acting to avoid that in the future. A wounded animal is more motivated than a slightly uncomfortable one.

Our perceptions of pleasure and pain are more powerful drivers than the actual things. When our brain is judging between what will be a pleasant or painful experience, it's working from scenarios that we *think* could result if we took a course of action. In other words, our *perceptions* of pleasure and pain are really what's driving the cart. And sometimes those perceptions can be flawed. In fact, they are mostly flawed, which explains our tendency to work against our own best interests.

I can think of no better example of this rule than jalapeño chapulines. They're a spicy, traditional Mexican snack that's tasty and low in carbs. By the way, "chapulines" means "grasshoppers." We're talking chili-flavored grasshoppers. The insects.

Now, you may have no firsthand knowledge of how grasshoppers taste. Maybe you've never tried them. But the *thought* of eating grasshoppers may give you pause. You imagine they'll be repellent to the tongue. You imagine if you take a bite of a grasshopper you'll get grossed out. You might accidentally bite down on an internal grasshopper organ. The *perception* of eating a grasshopper is driving you quickly away from the act of eating one.

But the fact remains that *you haven't actually tried it yet*. You're working from your *idea* of the repulsion that eating a grasshopper will bring about. Somebody who's actually tried grasshopper-based cuisine may insist to you that they're really *good* when prepared properly. Still, you might not be able to get over your innate perception of what eating an insect would be like.

Pleasure and pain are changed by time. In general, we focus on the here and now: what can I get very soon that will bring me happiness? Also, what is coming up very soon that could be intensely painful that I'll have to avoid? When considering the attainment of comfort, we're more tuned into what might happen immediately. The pleasure and pain that might happen months or years from now don't really register with us—what's most important is whatever's right at our doorstep. Of course, this is another way in which our perceptions are flawed and why we procrastinate so frequently, for example.

Suppose a smoker needs a cigarette. It's the main focus of their current situation. It brings them a certain relief or pleasure. And in about fifteen minutes, they'll be on break so they can enjoy that cigarette. It's the focus of their daily ritual. They're *not* thinking how smoking a cigarette every time they "need" one could cause painful health problems down the road. That's a distant reality that's not driving them at all. Right now, they need a smoke because they crave one, and they might get a headache immediately if they don't get one.

Emotion beats logic. When it comes to the pleasure principle, your feelings tend to overshadow rational thought. You might know that doing something will be good or bad for you. You'll understand all the reasons why it will be good or bad. You'll get all that. But if your illogical id is so intent on satisfying a certain craving, then it's probably going to win out. And if your id drives you to think that doing something useful will cause too much stress or temporary dissatisfaction, it's going to win there too.

Going back to our smoker, without a doubt they know why cigarettes are bad for one's health. They've read those warnings on the packages. Maybe in school they saw a picture of a corroded lung that resulted from years of smoking. They *know* all the risks they're about to court. But there's that pack right in front of them. And all reason be damned, they're going to have that cigarette. Their emotions oriented toward pleasure win out.

Survival overrides everything. When our survival instinct gets activated, everything else in our psychological and emotional makeup turns off. If a life-threatening situation (or a *perceived* life-threatening situation) arises in our existence, the brain closes down everything else and turns us into a machine whose thoughts and actions are all oriented toward the will to survive.

This shouldn't be surprising when it comes to avoiding painful outcomes. Of *course* you're going to try and jump away from that oncoming semi-truck; if you don't, you won't survive. Your system won't let you make that choice— it's going to do everything it can to get you the hell out of the way of that truck.

However, survival can *also* come into play when we're seeking pleasure—even if it means we might slip into harm's way. The most obvious example of this is food. Say you're at a bar and somebody orders a giant plate of nachos loaded with cheese, sour cream, fatty meat, and a bunch of other things that might not be the best dietary choices for you. You *might* be able to resist it. Some people can. But you might not. In fact, you could find yourself eating half the plate before you even know what you've done.

Why? Because you need food to survive. And your brain is telling you there's food in the vicinity, so perhaps you should eat it. Never mind that it's not the best kind of food, nutritionally speaking, that you could opt for at the moment. Your survival instinct is telling you it's time to have those nachos. Your life depends on it.

The pleasure principle is related to an idea that comes from economics and the attempt to predict markets and human buying behavior: the *rational choice theory*, embodied by the jokingly named *Homo economicus*. This states that all of our choices and decisions spring entirely from self-interest and the desire to bring as much pleasure to our lives as possible. It may not always hold up (otherwise market and stock prices would be 100% predictable), but it provides more support for the simple nature of many of our motivations.

What does someone have to gain or to avoid? This should provide a handy guide for reading people's actions. The next two models of motivation play indirectly on this idea that humans are always seeking or avoiding something.

The Pyramid of Needs

Maslow's hierarchy of needs is one of the most famous models in the history of psychology. It employs a pyramid to show how certain human "needs"—like food, sleep, and warmth—are necessary to resolve before more aspirational needs like love, accomplishment, and vocation. Maslow's pyramid can be viewed as a visual example of how motivation changes and increases after we get what we need at each stage in our lives, which typically coincides with where we are on the hierarchy itself.

When psychology professor Abraham Maslow came along in the 1940s, his theory boiled everything down to one revolutionary idea: human beings are a product of a set of basic human needs, the deprivation of which is the primary cause of most psychological problems. Fulfilling these needs is what drives us on a daily basis. What's more, these needs are ranked, and the fulfilment of some higher-order needs first requires the fulfilment of other, more foundational needs.

These basic needs are ranked, and those at the bottom must be fulfilled first, before those higher up on the list. Maslow's hierarchy of needs, now named for him, maps out basic human needs and desires and how they evolve throughout life. It functions like a ladder—if you aren't able to satisfy your more basic foundational human needs and desires, it is extremely difficult to move forward without stress and dissatisfaction in life. It means your motivations change depending on where you are in the hierarchy.

To illustrate, let's take a look at how our needs and associated motivations change from infancy to adulthood. As infants, we don't feel any need for a career or life satisfaction. We simply need to rest, be fed, and have shelter over our heads. Feeding and survival are our only real needs and desires (as parents of newborns will tell you).

As we grow from infants into teenagers, simply staying alive and healthy doesn't bring satisfaction. We hunger for interpersonal relationships and friendships. What drives us is to find a feeling of belonging and community. Then, as we mature into young adults, simply having a great group of friends is no longer enough to satisfy us. It feels empty, actually, without an overall sense of purpose.

If, as young adults, we are fortunate enough to be able to provide financial security and stability for ourselves and our families, then our desires and needs can turn outward rather than inward. It's the same reason that people like Warren Buffett and Bill Gates start participating in philanthropy to make as big an impact as they can on the world.

The stages of Maslow's hierarchy of needs determine exactly what you're motivated by depending on where you are in the hierarchy.

The first stage is physiological fulfillment. This is easily seen in the daily life of an infant. All that matters to them is that their basic needs for survival are met (i.e., food, water, and shelter). Without security in these aspects, it is difficult for anyone to focus on satisfaction in anything else—it would actually be harmful to them to seek other forms of satisfaction. So this is the baseline level of fulfillment that must first be met.

The second stage is safety. If someone's belly is full, they have clothes on their back, and they have a roof over their head, they need to find a way to ensure that those things keep on coming. They need to have a secure source of income or resources to increase the certainty and longevity of their safety. The first two stages are designed to ensure overall survival. Unfortunately, many people never make it out of these first two stages due to unfortunate circumstances, and you can plainly see why they aren't concerned with fulfilling their potential.

The third stage is love and belonging. Now that your survival is ensured, you'll find that it is relatively empty without sharing it with people that you care about. Humans are social creatures, and case studies have shown that living in isolation will literally cause insanity and mental instability, no matter how well fed or secure you are. This includes relationships with your friends and family and socializing enough so you don't feel that you are failing in your social life.

Of course, this stage is a major sticking point for many people—they are unable to be fulfilled or focus on higher desires because they lack the relationships that create a healthy lifestyle. Isn't it easy to imagine someone who is stuck at a low level of happiness because they don't have any friends?

The fourth stage is self-esteem. You can have relationships, but are they healthy ones that make you feel confident and supported?

This stage is all about how your interactions with others impact your relationship with yourself. This is a very interesting level of maturity in terms of needs because it boils down to self-acceptance. You know you have a healthy level of self-esteem when you can accept yourself even if you are misunderstood or outright disliked by others. For you to get to this stage and have a healthy level of self-esteem, you have to have accumulated certain achievements or earned the respect of others. There is a strong interplay between how you get along with others and help others and how you feel about yourself.

The final stage is self-actualization. The highest level of Maslow's hierarchy is self-actualization. This is when you are able to live for something higher than yourself and your needs. You feel that you need to connect with principles that require you to step beyond what is convenient and what is comfortable. This is the plane of morality, creativity, spontaneity, lack of prejudice, and acceptance of reality.

Self-actualization is placed at the top of the pyramid because this is the highest (and last) need people have. All the lower levels have to be met first, before a person can reach this last level. You know you are working with somebody who operates at a truly high level when they do not focus so much on what is important to them, their self-esteem, or how other people perceive them. This is the stage people are at when they say they want to find their calling and purpose in life.

Maslow's theory may not accurately describe all of our daily desires, but it does provide an inventory for the broad strokes of what we want in life. It also gives us a ranked framework to understand the importance of these needs relative to one another. We can observe people to understand which stage of life they are in, what is currently important to them, and what they require to get to the next level in the hierarchy.

McClelland's Model

As mentioned, David McClelland's Human Motivation Theory is also a helpful tool for understanding what people are motivated by and what that can tell us about them. Rather than looking at goals themselves, it's a question of what deeper emotional need may be satisfied by achieving that goal.

Primarily used in the workplace, this theory narrows down human needs to just three: the need for affiliation (social interaction and belonging), for power, and for achievement. Every one of us will prioritize one or two over the others. Because they're learned, these needs come primarily from early childhood experiences, family values, or cultural expectations. Let's consider each need and the kind of person who might experience each one predominantly.

First, the need for achievement is all about establishing and reaching goals. A person motivated by achievement lives for the moment they can succeed at a challenging task. This is the guy in the office who has no problem taking carefully considered risks—in fact, he may even seem to relish the excitement of a good test of his abilities. Such a person will prefer working alone, just them and their goal off in the distance, and they need regular feedback from others to motivate them as they progress on their missions. Imagine the person who loves running grueling marathons just to convince themselves they can. This motivation is behind many artists or entrepreneurs, explorers, inventors, businesspeople, and those who love a game or dare.

Those who are motivated by affiliation will act and think completely differently. Their main need is for the satisfaction, meaning, and sense of security that comes with belonging to the group. Unlike those motivated by achievement for its own sake, these people understand and like collaboration and group work. They want people to like them and don't want to participate in anything that doesn't flow harmoniously for all involved. Though they shy away from risk and competition, such a person shines in more complex social situations and can be extraordinarily effective in the name of group cohesion and agreement.

Lastly, those motivated by power are in turn completely different from the other two. The dominant need and desire is for influence over not just situations, but other people. Such a person will welcome competition much like the person motivated by achievement, but it's not the trophy or the satisfaction of completion that they care about—what is appealing is *winning*. Having a high status relative to others and being recognized as such is a strong motivating force for this person. Though they may also want to be liked just as the previous type does, it will be because they are superior in some way, not because being liked helps things run more smoothly in the group. The power need can be either interpersonal (control over others) or it can be institutional (control over an organization's proceedings).

Of course, real people are complicated and may have a combination of different drives and motivations, as well as having idiosyncratic ways of expressing those desires. We each live in different environments with different opportunities and limitations, and we've each experienced different life events. Furthermore, each of us may be more or less effective at getting those needs met, and the response we get from others may be strongly dependent on culture or context. Nevertheless, homing in on the one dominant motivator can be a powerful way of gaining clarity over someone's behavior.

In the workplace, this theory is used to understand how to give employees feedback and how to reward and discipline them. But it can be used out of the workplace, too, any time you need to answer the question, "Why is this person behaving like this?"

If you can, consider a person's past actions. Look carefully at the way they behave, what they say, who they interact with and how, what they seem to care about, and so on. Look also at what seems to bother them or be challenging for them. You can likely get a good idea of someone's core motivator this way.

Then consider what you need in your interactions with this person and strategize beforehand using what you know about *their* motivations. How best can you communicate with them so that your message is properly heard? How can you frame a request so that they are more likely to understand and work with you? If you want to praise them, what would they consider to be the ultimate compliment? And if something isn't working between the two of you, could it be because of your clashing perspectives?

Imagine you're trying to plan a surprise birthday party with a few family members. One of them barges ahead with planning before consulting anyone else. The other is upset by this and complains to you that they had other ideas. Knowing what you do about each of them, you quietly chat to the first and realize that, being strongly motivated by achievement, they've gone off independently to pursue the satisfaction of getting the party planning done quickly. When talking to the other family member, you guess they're more motivated by the need for affiliation, and want primarily for everyone to get along, in the planning and in the enjoyment of the party.

Respecting both of their orientations, you decide to ask the first family member to draw up a list of tasks that need to be done and set them to work on getting the best rates for venue hire, etc. You understand that they'll also want some positive feedback when they return from their "mission." For the other family member, you commit to working with them directly, knowing that they cherish collaboration and the experience of mutual effort toward a goal. You have a long chat over coffee with them and reassure them that their input is valued in the planning process, and you offer them the task of communicating with all the people invited to the party.

The more you can understand where people are coming from in terms of motivation, the better you'll be able to interact with them, understand them, and even manage conflict if necessary. Ultimately, motivations are nothing more than the sophisticated shapes our pleasure-seeking or pain avoidance takes. To understand *what* people are doing, it's useful to understand *why* they're doing it.

McClelland's theory is about motivations that are primarily toward something—power, achievement, affiliation—but we can also be equally motivated away from something. People act to increase certain feelings or get closer to what they value, but they also act to reduce pain or defend against what they don't value or are actively scared of. Of course, this is the pleasure principle in full glory.

Next, we move to a very important type of pain and discomfort that we are always motivated to avoid: damage to the ego.

Defense of the Ego

So far, we've considered needs and motivations that can be best described as aspirational, i.e., things we want to achieve, attain, and bring about in our lives. We could look at it in another way-a lot of what motivates people may come down to what they're most afraid of, and what they would do anything to avoid.

Protecting yourself from feelings of failure, inadequacy, shame, or inferiority is often seen as a powerful motivator of behavior. We are highly motivated to shield the ego for many reasons, mostly because we don't want to feel as though we are bad, useless, unwanted, unloved, unacceptable, or somehow less than others.

This all-too-human instinct may stem from the desire to feel important and relevant, or to know that we belong in the world and somehow have a place in our "tribe" with others like us. Whatever the reason, the ego's instinct to protect itself can be reality-bending and can cause mass intellectual dishonesty and self-deception. The ego can be like a massive black hole that distorts the social reality around it. As such, this makes it another highly predictable indicator we can use to analyze people's behavior.

Someone who's underperforming at work might feel the need to protect their perceived skills and talent by deflecting responsibility to "The boss has always had it in for me. And who trained me? Him! It's all his fault one way or another." Someone who trips and falls yet fancies themselves graceful will blame the fact that it rained six days ago, their shoes have no grip, and *who put that rock there anyway!*? Someone who fails to make the school basketball team will grumble that the coach hated them, they weren't used to that particular style of play, and they didn't *really* want to make the team anyway.

This is what it sounds like when the ego steps in to protect itself. There's so much justification and deflecting going on that it's difficult to know what is real and what is not.

This all stems from the universal truth that nobody likes to be wrong or to fail. It's embarrassing and confirms all of our worst anxieties about ourselves. Instead of accepting being wrong as a teachable moment or lesson, our first instinct is to run from our shame and cower in the corner. This is the same reason we will persist in an argument to the death, even if we know we are 100% wrong. If the ego had a physical manifestation, it would be sizable, sensitive, and heavily armored (to the point of going on the offensive)—essentially a giant porcupine.

When the ego senses danger, it has no interest or time to consider the facts. Instead, it seeks to alleviate discomfort in the quickest way possible. And that means you lie to yourself so you can keep the ego safe and sound. It also means we lie (to put it bluntly) to others, too.

We try to cover up the truth, deflect attention from it, or develop an alternative version that makes the actual truth seem less hurtful. We might boast a little, downplay certain unpleasant facts, fudge the numbers a little, put a little "spin" on things and in general use certain modes of "interpretation" that conveniently position us more or less on top. And it's right in that moment that intellectual dishonesty is born. Are any of those convoluted theories likely to withstand any amount of scrutiny? Probably not, but the problem is that the ego doesn't allow for acknowledgment and analysis of what really happened. It blinds you.

Let's be clear: these aren't lies that you dream up or concoct in advance. You do not *intend* to lie to yourself. You don't even *feel* they're lies. You may not even know you're doing it, as sometimes these defense mechanisms can occur unconsciously. They're not explicitly intellectually dishonest because you *want* to delude yourself. Rather, they're automatic strategies that the constantly neurotic ego puts into action because it's terrified of looking foolish or wrong. Unfortunately, that's the worst zone to be in, as it means *you don't know what you don't know.*

Over time, these ego-driven errors in thinking inform your entire belief system and give you rationalized justifications for almost everything. You never make any sports team because the coaches always hate you, and you keep failing the driving test because your hand-eye coordination is *uniquely special.*

These lies become your entire reality, and you rely on them to get yourself through problematic situations or to dismiss efforts to find the truth. We're not talking about just giving excuses for why you aren't a violin virtuoso; this manner of thinking can become the factors that drive your decisions, thinking, and evaluations of anything and anyone.

So if you're struggling to understand someone who doesn't appear to be able to utter the words "I'm wrong," now you know exactly what's going on in their head. They may not know, but at least you are able to analyze them more deeply.

Let's take Fred. Fred was an ardent fan of a pop star his whole life. He grew up listening to his music and formed a lot of his identity around his admiration for him. We're talking an entire bedroom wall filled with posters of this star and outfits that were replicas of this star's clothes hanging in his closet.

Late in his career, this pop star was put on trial for a serious crime. Fred steadfastly stood by his pop star idol, even as lurid details of his case were reported by courtroom reporters to the press. "Nobody I admire this way would ever be guilty of this," Fred said. "It's all just a conspiracy put together by the people who resent him for whatever reason."

The pop star was ultimately found guilty and sentenced to multiple years in prison. Fred had shown up outside the courthouse bearing a sign that protested his star's innocence. Even as compelling evidence was eventually released to the press, Fred maintained that the pop star was absolutely innocent, dismissing all of the victims' claims by protesting that they were "jealous" and "just trying to get the spotlight themselves."

Why would Fred continue to insist, against all reasonable and provable evidence, that his idol was innocent? Because his ego was so wrapped up in his worship of the pop star that it was predisposed to consider him blameless. For him to believe the truth would have meant a devastating blow to almost everything he believed in (*I worship a criminal? What does that say about me?*), and the ego wasn't going to let that happen for a minute—even if it meant making him deny what was fairly compelling and unshakable proof that the star was guilty.

In your pursuit of truth and clear thought, your ego will rear its ugly head like the enraged porcupine. It has set up a series of tactical barriers to keep you from learning something that might upset your belief system, and it is only after you can rein in your ego that you are open to learning. After all, you can't defend yourself and listen at the same time.

Defense mechanisms are the specific ways we protect our ego, pride, and self-esteem. These methods keep us whole when times are tough. The origin of the term comes from Sigmund Freud.

These so-called defense mechanisms are also a powerful predictor of behavior and will give you a deep insight into why people do what they do. Defense mechanisms can take many varied and colorful forms, but there are a few common patterns that you'll see in others (and hopefully yourself!). These psychological shields rear up when the ego senses something it doesn't agree with, can't face, or wishes wasn't true.

Loss, rejection, uncertainty, discomfort, humiliation, loneliness, failure, panic... all of these can be defended against using certain mental tricks. These mechanisms are there to protect us from experiencing negative emotions. They work in the moment, but in the long run, they are ineffective since they rob us of the opportunity to face, accept, and digest inevitably negative emotions as they crop up.

Naturally, if you can observe somebody using a defense mechanism, you can instantly infer a lot about them and their world, particularly about the things they find themselves unable to deal with. This in turn tells you a lot about how they see themselves, their strengths and weaknesses, and what they value. Let's look at some defense mechanisms with concrete examples. You just might recognize these two defense mechanisms put forth by his daughter, Anna Freud: denial and rationalization.

Denial is one of the most classic defense mechanisms because it is easy to use. Suppose you discovered that you were performing poorly at your job. "No, I don't believe that report ranking all of the employees. There's no way I can be last. Not in this world. The computer added up the scores incorrectly."

What is true is simply claimed to be false, as if that makes everything go away. You are acting as if a negative fact doesn't exist. Sometimes we don't realize when we do this, especially in situations that are so dire they actually appear fantastical to us.

All you have to do is say "no" often enough and you might begin to believe yourself, and that's where the appeal of denial lies. You are actually changing your reality, where other defense mechanisms merely spin it to be more acceptable. This is actually the most dangerous defense mechanism, because even if there is a dire problem, it is ignored and never fixed. If someone continued to persist in the belief they were an excellent driver, despite a string of accidents in the past year, it's unlikely they would ever seek to practice their driving skills.

Rationalization is when you explain away something negative.

It is the art of making excuses. The bad behavior or fact still remains, but it is turned into something unavoidable because of circumstances out of your control. The bottom line is that anything negative is not your fault and you shouldn't be held accountable for it. It's never a besmirching of your abilities. It's extremely convenient, and you are only limited by your imagination.

Building on the same prior example of poor job performance, this is easily explained away by the following: your boss secretly hating you, your coworkers plotting against you, the computer being biased against your soft skills, unpredictable traffic affecting your commute, and having two jobs at once. These flimsy excuses are what your ego needs to protect itself.

Rationalization is the embodiment of the *sour grapes fable*. A fox wanted to reach some grapes at the top of a bush, but he couldn't leap high enough. To make himself feel better about his lack of leaping ability, and to comfort himself about his lack of grapes, he told himself the grapes looked sour anyway, so he wasn't missing out on anything. He was still hungry, but he'd rather be hungry than admit his failure.

Rationalization can also help us feel at peace with poor decisions we've made with phrases such as "It was going to happen at some point anyway." Rationalization ensures you never have to face failure, rejection, or negativity. It's always someone else's fault!

While comforting, where do reality and truth go amidst all of this? Out the window, mostly. Intellectual honesty requires you to first defeat your natural tendencies to be dishonest. Thoughts dictated by self-protection don't overlap with clear, objective thoughts.

Closely associated is **repression**. Whereas in denial the reality is refused or downright rejected, repression is where a person pushes the thought or feeling so far out of consciousness they "forget" it. It's as though the threatening emotion never existed in the first place. An example might be the child above who experiences abuse. Because it is so painful, and because they had no way of helping themselves, they might push the memory so far away that they never have to deal with it.

Sometimes, the overpowering emotion is unwelcome, but what is really unacceptable to the ego is *where* it comes from. In such a case,

displacement might occur as a protection against unpleasant truths. A woman might work at a job she hates but cannot realistically leave. Simply, she cannot express or even acknowledge that she resents her job because this draws a threatening attention to her financial bind. What she might do, though, is take that resentment and put it elsewhere. She might come home every day and kick the dog or yell at her children, convinced that they are the ones making her angry. It is easier and less risky to confront her feelings of anger when they are directed at her pets or children.

Projection is a defense mechanism that can cause considerable damage and chaos if not understood for what it is. In this case, we place unwanted and unclaimed feelings onto someone or something else rather than seeing that they are a part of ourselves. We do not recognize our own "dark side" and project it onto others, blaming them for our shortcomings or seeing our flaws in their actions.

An example is a man who is cheating on his wife. He finds his own behavior unacceptable, but rather than allow himself to condemn his own actions, he projects that shame onto his (bewildered) partner and is suddenly suspicious of her behavior, accusing *her* of keeping something from *him*.

The example of a blatantly homophobic man who is revealed to later be gay is so common by now it's almost comical. **Reaction formation** just might be behind it. Whereas denial simply says, "This isn't happening," reaction formation goes a step further and claims, "Not only is that not happening, but the exact opposite is the case. Look!"

A woman might be terrified of her new cancer diagnosis and, rather than admit her fear, puts on a show to everyone of being courageous, preaching to others about how death is nothing to fear.

In times of extreme emotional distress, you might find yourself *regressing* to a simpler time (i.e., childhood). When you were young, life was easier and less demanding—to cope with threatening emotions, many of us return there, acting "childish" as a way to cope. A man might be facing some legal troubles over misfiled taxes. Rather than face the situation, he gets into a screaming match with his accountant, banging his fists on the table in a "tantrum" and then pouting when people try to reason with him.

Finally, we come to **sublimation**. In the same way that projection and displacement take the negative emotions and place them elsewhere, sublimation takes that emotion and channels it through a different, more acceptable outlet. A single man might find the loneliness at home unbearable and channels that unmet need into doing charity work four nights a week. A woman may receive some bad news, but rather than get upset, she goes home and proceeds to do a massive spring clean of her home. A person might routinely turn panic and anxiety into a dedication to prayer, and so on.

Defense of the ego is a nasty habit, but it's easy to recognize when you know of its insidious presence. Sometimes we can't help it; we're all human. But we can use this to our advantage by using it as a clear quantity to analyze people with.

Takeaways:

- We've talked about analyzing and predicting behavior based on people's emotions and values, but what about motivation? It turns out there are a few prominent and fairly universal models of motivation that can give you a helpful framework to understand people with. When you can pinpoint what people are motivated by, you can see how everything leads back to it either directly or indirectly.
- Any discussion on motivation must begin with the pleasure principle, which generally

states that we move toward pleasure and move away from pain. If you think about it, this is omnipresent in our daily lives in both minuscule and huge ways. As such, this actually makes people more predictable to understand. What is the pleasure people are seeking, and what is the pain they are avoiding? It's always there in some way.

- Next, we move to the pyramid of needs, otherwise known as Abraham Maslow's hierarchy of needs. It states that we are all seeking various types of needs in various points in our lives; when you can observe which level other people are in, you can understand what they are seeking out and motivated by. The levels of the hierarchy are as follows: physiological fulfillment, safety, love and belonging, self-esteem, and self-actualization. Of course, this model, as well as the next one, also functions based on the pleasure principle.

- David McClelland's model of motivation has only three aspects (though they are broader) than Maslow's hierarchy of needs: affiliation (social interaction and belonging), power, and achievement. Similarly, you can deduce what is motivating people by their actions relatively easily.

- Finally, we come to defense of the ego. This is one of our most powerful motivators, but it is mostly unconscious. Simply put, we act to guard our ego from anything that would make us feel psychologically *less*. In doing so, it is so powerful that it allows us to bend reality and lie to ourselves and others—all outside of our conscious awareness. Defense mechanisms are the ways that we avoid responsibility and negative feelings, and they include denial, rationalization, projection, sublimation, regression, displacement, repression, and reaction formation, to name a few. When you know the ego is in play, it often takes front stage over other motivations.

Chapter 7. Remnants of the Past

Nobody really knows the future. But sometimes, knowing what's already happened is a powerful way of predicting what may happen next. Though people are far more complex than billiard balls on a table, they nevertheless are influenced by events in the past; their current behavior is a natural extension of what's come before. If you can learn to interpret the past well, you can gain a more thorough understanding of people's actions, motivations, and worldviews right now in the present.

Occurrences in the past can set up predictable patterns of behavior. Though nobody would argue that they're an individual with a unique will and life path, it's a fact that we are all influenced by our upbringings, early childhood experiences, and key events in our past. Freud might seem a little bizarre to our modern tastes, but he was essentially right in acknowledging the enormous effect early childhood has on the adult personality.

It's easiest to see it in others: nobody really stops to think that they're busy having a particular worldview. They merely think, "This is the way the world works because it's what I experienced growing up, and it's what my parents told me." Without a second thought, they let those assumptions drive their expectations, goals, actions, and feelings about themselves. If you can understand the themes and challenges of someone's life story, you can understand *them*, not as people with fixed traits but as living, evolving beings that respond and move with their circumstances in predictable ways.

What's Your Attachment?

Attachment theory is one of the most prominent theories of how unconscious happenings during childhood affect people well into adulthood—relationships and perception of yourself to others in this case.

Based on research started by John Bowlby, notably continued by Mary Ainsworth, then by Bartholomew and Horowitz, there are four main attachment styles, or ways we approach emotional attachment to other people. These patterns usually begin with children's relationships with their parents or caretakers and persist into adulthood, where they influence adult relationships. Our parents show us a model of how the world works, and this is for better or worse. We are helpless to abide by it unless we are made aware and actively fight against it.

According to Bowlby, children are constantly assessing the presence and attentiveness of their caretaking figure. If the child perceives them to be available and supportive, he will feel loved, secure, and confident. As a result, the child will feel confident to explore and have a degree of physical and mental separation from the caretaker.

This is a dynamic that will inform his relationships for the rest of his life. However, if the child perceives that the caretaking figure is distracted, unavailable, or unreliable, the child will experience anxiety and become fearful whenever the caretaker is not in his immediate vicinity. These feelings form the basis for the attachment styles, and they do persist into adulthood and influence our actions in many ways—romantic or otherwise.

Eventually, four patterns, or attachment styles, became articulated.

- secure

- anxious-preoccupied
- dismissive-avoidant
- fearful-avoidant

Secure Attachment. As much as we would like to think that secure attachment is the most common attachment style, it absolutely is not. And there's a reason the other three attachment styles have somewhat ominous names.

People with secure attachment styles are emotionally balanced and have a history of warm and caring interactions that began in childhood. They don't approach people with a sense of fear. Instead, they have a strong sense of self and look for the positive in any relationship.

They have a healthy range of positive and negative emotions and are less prone to emotional outbursts because they don't need to assume the worst. They may be independent or relatively dependent, but it's a conscious choice and not based on anxiety or fear. Of course, this all stems from healthy and secure interactions with their primary caretakers.

Securely attached people feel comfortable with intimacy. They do not view it as a threat or as something that can lull them into a false sense of security, only to be taken away. Not surprisingly, these people are able to be genuinely open and loving. The biggest difference between securely attached people and other types of people is their lack of insecurity. This allows them to open themselves up to others yet give others space when it is needed.

They are not jealous or possessive and they don't have nightmares about being cheated on. They are attentive but relaxed and generally allow independence and freedom because they don't feel they have anything to worry about.

Don't make the mistake of assuming that your attachment style is automatically secure or healthy. If you don't take the time to diagnose yourself, and you subsequently attempt to remedy or fix a problem with your relationships, it's like taking a random medication to treat an illness. It doesn't make sense to do that. And yes, loving others does indeed start with loving yourself.

Anxious-Preoccupied Attachment. This is the first type of insecure attachment, and it is defined by anxiety and preoccupation with the relationship. It's important to keep in mind that all of the insecure or anxious styles of attachment spring from an absent caretaking figure.

People with this attachment style tend to fixate on whether their partner loves them as much as they love their partner. It is a constant source of anxiety for them because they can never be adequately reassured. Every small sign that could possibly be interpreted as negative is unequivocally negative to them and causes them significant mental anguish. They tend to measure this on a daily basis, which causes undue stress.

At the heart of it, people with this attachment style are very insecure and don't regard themselves in a very positive light. They doubt that their partner is able to love them in a true and genuine way. There is an inferiority complex at work here, and constant validation is required in any and all forms.

Their anxiety goes into remission when they are in close contact with their paramour, so they naturally want more and more. Interestingly, they focus mainly on the love they are receiving, not the love they are giving to their partner. This is a serious problem because the classic definition of love, of course, is a person *giving*.

By many accounts, true love is measured by what you provide, what you sacrifice, and the emotional value you give to another person. This begs the question—do people with this attachment style feel true love, or is a relationship merely a vehicle to validate their self-worth?

Dismissive-Avoidant Attachment. Dismissive-avoidant people are focused on protecting their independence in their relationships, which can sound a bit like an oxymoron.

They are afraid that once they get into a relationship or close friendship, they will become saddled with duties and obligations and lose control of their life. They are happy with the fact that they are able to make choices in the first place and are fierce about protecting that privilege. They conflate deep levels of emotional intimacy with a loss of independence and control.

To that effect, they don't feel the need for close emotional relationships because they appear to do more bad than good for them. They characterize themselves as islands or lone wolves by choice. Their very predictable response is to minimize closeness. They come up with arrangements to keep people at arm's length. It is not uncommon for dismissive-avoidant people to set ground rules that prevent the relationship from truly maturing.

Avoidant people take great pains to minimize true emotional closeness and thus vulnerability. It is not because they do not love the other person, but they perceive strong emotional attachment as something that will rob them of their independence, so they choose to defend themselves. They don't lack empathy; they just don't let it dictate their actions.

People with this style of attachment sometimes suppress their emotions because of how independent they characterize themselves. They have a very doubtful view of relationships and close friendships, so it's unclear if you'd be able to get them into one. They have a strong fight-or-flight response—meaning that if things don't go their way, they will often prioritize themselves first and leave the relationship.

They can be very difficult to deal with for other attachment styles because their style of attachment is to *not* have attachment. When someone wants to remain by themselves, it can be a waste of time trying to introduce your needs to them.

Fearful-Avoidant Attachment. At first glance, this attachment style appears similar to the dismissive-avoidant, but the dismissive-avoidant is motivated by very different things. They want to avoid emotional attachment because they feel attachments weaken them; they're a waste of time.

Fearful-avoidant people avoid emotional attachment because they feel attachment only leads to heartbreak, disappointment, and feelings of abandonment. Recall that these attachment styles often have their roots in childhood, so people with this attachment style may have experienced childhood traumas or abuse; they may have been abandoned or betrayed by someone they wanted or needed to depend on.

Despite wanting intimate relationships and emotional connection, they have issues opening up and truly getting close to others because a defensive wall shoots up that has been necessary in the past. Vulnerability has hurt them before and they want to prevent that now and in the future.

They do not have a positive view of others and have trouble seeing others as particularly trustworthy. Even if you have no history of wrongdoing and say all the right things, you will be constantly scrutinized by people with this attachment style. They are masters of preemptively rejecting others before they have the possibility of being hurt by them.

Because they want to protect themselves at all costs, they are uncomfortable displaying affection, verbal or otherwise. They suppress any positive feelings to keep themselves within the moat of their castle, and it can be tough to truly draw them out. It may take months or years to earn their trust, something they don't give easily. Constant affirmation and validation is necessary, and any opposing signals can make them want to bolt for safety.

We can use this knowledge of attachment styles to analyze people based on their actions. We can surmise exactly how they tend to feel about relationships and close friendships and, more importantly, how they treat those people. Attachment styles are one of the strongest footprints left by our upbringings. Unfortunately, you've noticed that three of the four attachment styles are negative in a way. The sad truth is that negativity often makes a more powerful impact, and thus we move to the effects of damaging parental patterns and how they can help us analyze others.

Parental Patterns and Self-Esteem

Naturally, negative patterns in early life have incredible power to shape a growing child. Typically, challenges that happen while a child is still learning about who they are can profoundly affect the development of self-esteem, identity, confidence, and security in oneself and the world at large.

Basically, self-esteem is our inner appraisal of our own worth as employees, partners, family members, and simply human beings. How we estimate our value as people is a complicated blend of perceiving our actions, thoughts, feelings, and relationships to others. Importantly, self-esteem is highly subjective and can be wildly "inaccurate" in the sense that a person can have a warped self-perception.

This is because we aren't born with the ability to be self-aware, and before we develop the skill of self-perception and self-appraisal, *others* are perceiving and appraising us. To develop this ability properly, a child needs caregivers to "mirror" back their experiences and validate them. You can already see how vulnerable this process might be!

Because we come into the world dependent on our caregivers, their judgments and reactions to us can have far-reaching consequences for the way we judge ourselves later on. We in effect internalize their opinions as our own, in the same way that a growing sapling will eventually take the shape of a container it's placed inside. If the key people in our lives mirror back to us a distorted appraisal of who we are, we don't challenge it—we accept it as fact and take it as our own.

Of course, this can have huge ramifications for our adult lives, influencing our thoughts, feelings, behaviors, and entire worldviews. We may over- or underestimate our worth—or perhaps a volatile combination of both! Now, if you can understand the roots of where low self-esteem comes from, you can better appreciate why people often feel worthless and how to approach this (very common) issue right now, in the present.

Let's look at some examples. You might encounter a person who you know grew up in a household where the parents were both successful overachievers and the children were always pushed quite hard to compete, to earn accolades, and to make their parents proud. On the surface, this perfectionism may seem harmless or even inspiring to others. An adult who grew up in such a home environment may well go on to earn great success in the world, and you could be forgiven for thinking they're rightly confident and pleased in their worth.

But dig only a little and you may see that the childhood trauma of constantly being made to feel "not good enough" drastically damages self-esteem. You might find that such a person doesn't even feel worthy of expressing how empty and unworthy they really feel. As soon as they reach a goal, they set another one, unable to ever stop and acknowledge that they have any worth as a person. If you know that someone had extremely demanding parents, try to understand that the message they received from their caregivers as vulnerable children was that they were not good enough, no matter what they did.

Does this person's workaholic attitude suddenly make sense? Can you understand why they feel like an "imposter"?

In another household, parents might not have been critical and demanding of their children but instead set their children up as their own caregivers in a reversal of roles. A mother who says to her upset child "Why are you doing this to *me*?" immediately communicates that the child's main value is only in relation to the mother's needs. When children's needs are not met or even acknowledged, and their parents teach them to sacrifice their own expression, preferences, and wants to their own or to other family members, it's like seeing no reflection when you look in the mirror.

Rather than feeling "not good enough," such a child may simply feel invisible and erased completely. Has somebody ever told you that growing up they were the de facto mother for all their younger siblings? Or that they had to take care of sick parents at a young age? Though such a person might derive a lot of their identity from being selfless and compassionate, you may also start to see patterns of weak boundaries, poor self-esteem, people-pleasing, and the inability to self-care.

Such a person may in fact feel that they barely even exist unless they are serving someone else. They may become "doormats" or vulnerable to abuse because their worldview runs on a core belief of "I am only worthwhile when I make others happy."

In yet a third household, imagine parents who, consciously or unconsciously, teach their child that they are unworthy of love. Nobody does this directly, obviously. Rather, the message comes through in small daily ways that come together to create a self-concept that doesn't amount to much. A father who tells a sick or frightened child that they're being silly and that there's nothing wrong will cement the attitude that they do not deserve care and attention. That father may himself model a lack of self-care and teach his children that emotions are unimportant and that expressing or nurturing them is indulgent and weak.

An adult who was raised in this environment will have difficulty caring for themselves in exactly the same way. Because their core belief tells them they are not important enough to get their needs met, they may delay taking themselves to the doctor or engage in poor lifestyle habits that undermine their well-being.

In this way, someone who was neglected in childhood may go on to neglect themselves in adulthood, even to the point of self-sabotage and self-destruction.

On the other end of the spectrum, you can also imagine a household where the parents are overly involved in the child's life, to such an extent that the child becomes psychologically dependent on that input. Children are more sensitive to their caregiver's perceptions of them, but at some point they need to develop their own self-concept, regardless of others' opinions or validation.

Caregivers can encourage this over-sensitivity to external appraisals of value by being inconsistent with praise, overly focused on social approval, or downright abusive. A mother might enter her daughter in countless beauty pageants, reinforcing again and again how important it is that everybody likes and approves of the girl's dress, hair, behavior, etc. She constantly asks, "What would other people think if they saw you now?" when the daughter misbehaves.

This could encourage a sense of self-worth that is conditional on external praise. A person raised this way will seek approval or go to great lengths to avoid disapproval. They may appear to have high self-esteem so long as everyone likes them, but the moment they receive criticism or are ignored, their sense of worth comes crashing down and they can feel incredibly empty and without value.

This leads to a final kind of trauma that has the opposite result as the examples above: the adult who has developed an overly inflated appraisal of their own worth as a result of early childhood traumas. Those who are classified as having narcissistic personality disorder show all the familiar traits: superficial charm, being absorbed in themselves and thinking of other people merely as objects or tools to get what they want, manipulation, gargantuan ego, being super concerned with status, winning and having power over others, a lack of empathy, and an attitude that they are perfect and incapable of doing anything wrong. But narcissism (though it really doesn't endear itself to others!) is a disorder that is also characterized by deep insecurity and shame.

The over-the-top confidence can be thought of as a defense mechanism on the scale of a personality. To combat poor emotional regulation, the inability to tolerate distress, and the sheer terror of facing feelings of deep worthlessness, a narcissist will construct an identity that is bulletproof, perfect, and impervious to pain.

Causes of narcissism can be complex, but in the very early stages of development of the self, the reflection given back to a narcissist is warped, and it's this warped sense of self that becomes internalized. Over-praising together with unpredictable care and high but unclear expectations can all play a part, as can parents who are insensitive to their children's inner world and value only the external. Criticism and abuse can cause a child to believe "I am only worthy when I'm the best" and act accordingly.

Regardless of exactly *how* these childhood experiences and traumas shape a growing individual, understanding that they *are* shaped this way sheds a whole new light on their behavior. If behavior is directly informed by the way we see ourselves and the world around us, then understanding how we see ourselves (i.e., our self-esteem) can offer insight into why we behave as we do.

Of course, early childhood experiences don't have to be limited only to neglect, abuse, or trauma. Our primary caregivers' influence on us is a given; the only question is the form this takes. Positive or even neutral events can impact our developing personalities just the same as negative ones. A classic example of a neutral circumstance that may have lasting effects on our personalities is birth order.

Which Child Are You?

Psychologists in the late '50s and early '60s started to popularize the idea that first-, middle-, and last-born children all differed from one another in predictable ways. That birth order is linked to personality seemed intuitively true to many parents: first-born children often seemed to mature faster and act more responsibly, youngest children were sometimes a bit naughty, etc.

But is there any evidence to support the theory? Though many might wish it were true, it turns out that, over time, researchers have actually not been able to gather much in the way of proof that birth order has a say on people's adult characteristics. Nevertheless, occasionally surprising studies do crop up and confirm our hunches that birth order might play a role after all.

The idea is not just that parents treat children in different ways, causing them to develop differently, but also that there is something inherent in the family position itself that encourages certain traits over others. Each child, by virtue of where they are relative to other children, will face unique challenges that in turn foster certain personality traits. Thus, a person telling you they're the "baby" of a family of five may be telling you something about their intelligence, their personality, and maybe even their sexual orientation.

Let's consider first-born children. Their parents necessarily are newbies at parenting. These children may end up enjoying very diligent and dedicated attention, since parents may be worried about getting things wrong. They may be overly attentive, a little neurotic, adoring, and very detail-oriented with their first born, and as a result, this child grows up very conscientious, cautious, and perhaps a bit of a control freak.

First-born children are said to be high achievers and ever so slightly more intelligent than later children (much to the chagrin of baby brothers and sisters the world over). Their reliable and organized attitudes make them mature for their age, and they mix well with adults—after all, they may have been the only babies in their world for a long time. Because they get their parents' undivided attention and the full force of their first-time-parent energy, these children are often primed to succeed in life.

Of course, there are challenges. All that perfectionism may mean first-born children are very hard on themselves, taking life seriously and not forgiving themselves easily if they feel they've failed. Being diligent and organized is great, but it can also translate to inflexibility, over-cautiousness, and being a little bossy with those around them (again, much to the chagrin of younger siblings).

The burden of being perfect allegedly makes first-born types dutiful and high achieving but prone to anxiety and control issues—the classic "Type A" stress bunnies. If you are one or have known first-born children, this portrait may resonate. You can easily imagine a group of children at home, the eldest acting as the self-appointed babysitter and threatening to tattle to Mom and Dad if one of the youngest breaks the rules.

This is the person whose parents sent them to all the extramurals and sports after school, who bought the baby Mozart CDs, and who still had energy to read books every night and take monthly visits to the museum. It's not difficult to imagine that parents, equal parts thrilled and terrified with their first child, would have subtly communicated to that child that the stakes were very high indeed and that Mom and Dad would be waiting in the wings, watching, hoping the child would achieve great things. It's a lot of pressure, isn't it?

And then, so the theory goes, some of that pressure dissipates by the time the next child comes along. The expert baby books have been set aside and there is less trial and error now. Mom and Dad are usually more comfortable and confident in their ability to raise a child—they've done it already! Consequently, they have a more relaxed and more permissive attitude the second time around.

There's less overall seriousness in raising the second child—less attentiveness. What's more, there may well be fewer resources and parents may be a little short on time too. How does this feel to child number two? The theory suggests that such a child will perceive and respond to this drop in attentiveness and be keenly aware of the fact that they're not the star of the show. In fact, they never were, unlike their older sibling, who at least for a time was the center of Mom and Dad's world.

This might manifest itself in attention-seeking behavior and a child who people-pleases, knowing that, deep down, parental affection is a bit of a competition for limited resources. While this child may have a very level-headed and humble view of himself, this can also show itself as low self-esteem. In multiple-child homes, they may suffer with identity problems. They're not the older leaders, they're not the youngest who need babying, but they're somewhere in between—and liable to be forgotten.

While the first child had the liberty of growing and developing alone and at their own pace, middle child will start to define themselves in relation to the other children. This immediate sense of the hierarchical nature of family life might make them a little rebellious. In multiple-children homes, middle children end up forming strong bonds with one another and later on grow into adults with strong social networks and good friendships. They are less likely to take on the parenting role to others or in turn want to be "babied."

They go with the flow, having learned to compromise early on and can be very agreeable, always understanding how to "fit in" and get along. They're also the most likely to become independent earlier on compared to their siblings. Middle kids at some point get to be the baby of the family, but all are eventually replaced by a new baby, and this lurking worry that their needs might go unmet may follow them into adulthood.

And then comes the last and final child. The theory tells us that, by this point, parents are far more laid-back about raising children. After all, they've been in the trenches and are far more relaxed and hands-off. A youngest child comes into a home already filled with people, including parents who are experienced, older, wiser, and a lot calmer. In fact, many older siblings can also play the role of surrogate parents as well, with the effect that the youngest child feels safe, enclosed, and generally looked after.

The result? These children are meant to be innocent, uncomplicated, and joyful. With outgoing personalities (they will have been passed around doting family members since day one) and the self-assurance that comes with knowing you can often get away with murder with a smile, youngest children keep something of the "baby" with them even as adults.

Youngest children are said to be charismatic, sociable, and crave the limelight. They love playing the clown and are often drawn to the stage, to performances, or to highly sociable professions where their warmth and likableness endear them to others. There's something about being the youngest in a family that makes you a little more free-spirited and adventurous than all those adults and older kids with chores to do. If you're the youngest, you may well have grown up watching others get into trouble for things you didn't, or being exempt from hard work just because you were too little.

The dark side of this personality type is obvious: youngest children may be a little manipulative with others, take unnecessary risks, or behave in self-centered or irresponsible ways. They may lack self-discipline and feel deep down that there's no real way for them to be original—after all, by the time they come along, their parents have already raised other children and may feel harder to impress or engage.

Again, it's worth remembering that birth order is simply one of many factors that can influence our personalities; though there's probably some truth in the birth order theory, people are complex and birth order alone will seldom account for somebody's personality perfectly.

How Parenting Styles Shape People as Adults

There is one final dimension we can explore when it comes to understanding an individual's upbringing, and that's the style of parenting they've received. By understanding the way a person was raised, you can get a glimpse into the kind of influences they might have experienced during their formative years. This in turn tells you a lot about how they view the world, themselves, and other people, as well as how they manage stress and criticism, what they do in conflicts, and how they manage themselves in relationships.

Our analysis can go two ways: by observing people's personalities, we can make conjectures about the kind of parenting they received in the past; on the other hand, if we know the parenting they received, we can make some educated guesses about the kind of people they may be today, as adults.

There is now plenty of research outlining roughly four parenting types:

1. Authoritarian
2. Permissive
3. Uninvolved
4. Authoritative

Let's take a quick look at each. You may find it easy to spot your own parents from this line-up, but try also to consider the possible parenting styles of other people you know. Can you spot any broader social, historic, or cultural patterns?

Authoritative parenting style

Most common in the 50s and often considered "traditional", this type of strict parenting positions the parent as the absolute authority and the child as subservient–or else. No-nonsense parents of this kind can be restrictive, demanding total obedience of the rules and regulations. Disobedience is punished. For such parents, their role is to be "the boss", and they tend to have little patience for silliness, preferring to leave childish things to children.

Permissive parenting style

This is in direct contrast to the above; the permissive parent would never say, "I'm your parent, not your friend" but would wish to reverse that and take on the role of a peer rather than an authority. There may be a marked lack of discipline, structure, order, or rules, and kids may take advantage of this to some degree. They seldom respect such parents, and chaos may rule the household.

Uninvolved parenting style

This is the style characterized by little effort taken towards meeting the child's needs. This may be outright neglect in terms of safety, food, and shelter, but can also be an overly disengaged or absent emotional attitude. These are the "hands-off" parents who are simply not present, and do not get involved with activities, preferring to leave their children to essentially raise themselves.

Authoratative parenting style

Contrasted to authoritarian, this parenting style is about healthy balance. The ideal is a parent who can set rules and boundaries, but also make efforts to meet a child's emotional needs and occasionally relax the structures of discipline if necessary.

These parents set rules but always take their children's feelings and unique needs into account. They use discipline, but this is more likely to be based on reward than on punishment, i.e., they attempt to instil a genuine appreciation for the meaning behind doing the right thing, rather than plain fear of punishment if they disobey.

As you can imagine, these different parenting styles can have profoundly different influences on children as they grow up and develop their personalities and coping styles. Authoritarian, permissive, and uninvolved parents tend to create anxious, avoidant, or disorganized attachment styles in their children. Healthy attachment styles are more characteristic of people raised by authoritative parents.

In the context of people-reading, how can we guess what style of upbringing a person has had? We can consider all the traces of the past that linger on in the present:

People raised by authoritarian parents may be consistently unhappy or unassertive/subservient adults. They can have complicated relationships with authority, or experience depression and anxiety. Because they are so used to being dominated or even bullied, they may be insecure and hypersensitive, tending to internalize relationship problems. They often assume that all conflict is because there's something wrong with them as people. Occasionally, authoritarian parents can actually end up encouraging deceitful, avoidant behavior since they heavily incentivize their children to give only the *appearance* of obedience.

Authoritarian parenting can sometimes instil in a child the very same authoritarian values, leading to adults who are also image-obsessed, anxious about status, and preoccupied with achievement. To cope with being bullied by their parents, they may find others to bully in turn, perhaps even their own children (Kim et. al., 2021, *Association of Parent–child Experiences with Insecure Attachment in Adulthood: A Systematic Review and Meta-analysis*).

Permissive parents can raise children who grow up to display all sorts of behavioral problems stemming from low impulse control. Growing up without structure and stability, they may struggle with obesity and consistent self-care, and may fail to establish their own healthy habits as adults.

Uninvolved parents can raise children who eventually struggle with self-esteem, or who feel chronically unseen and unheard in life as adults. They may "fall in with a bad crowd" or have trouble finding their own stability in employment or relationships. Occasionally, they can become the overly responsible but joyless types, especially if they have had to take on a more adult role for younger siblings. Either way, there tends to be an avoidant attachment style and a fear of rejection and abandonment that can seriously undermine the health of future adult relationships (Hyun, 2019).

All three of the above parenting styles can result in adults who display

- Self-sabotaging behavior
- Increased risk of getting into relationships with narcissists
- Perfectionism and compulsive behaviors
- Critical self-talk
- Overthinking and catastrophic rumination
- An inability to feel safe in relationships; trust issues
- Feelings of shame and unworthiness
- Isolation
- An extremely judgmental attitude
- Low self-esteem and body image issues

- Higher risk of alcohol use, obesity, or self-medicating behaviors
- Loner behavior, avoiding asking for help (Kiviniemi, et al., 2020).

Authoratative parents tend to raise the happiest and most well-adjusted children of all. If there is a healthy balance between discipline and care, a child can grow into an adult that copes well, takes responsibility, but also has enough self-esteem and resilience. The hallmark of such a childhood is the ability to self-regulate as an adult.

As fascinating as all this is, how can we use it to better understand the adults we encounter in our lives? Knowledge about parenting styles is best used to help you understand broader psychological patterns. By extending your working model of an individual's personality into the past, you give yourself a richer, more three-dimensional view of not just who they are, but *why* they are that way. Here are a few questions to ask when you're analysing someone and gathering data:

In the first instance, **notice how they talk about their own parents,** as well as how they respond to other parents, even if they're just fictional or hypothetical. The way people talk about parents in general tells you a lot about their experiences. What is their predominant emotion when recalling memories about their own parents? Is it fear, admiration, love, or indifference? This is a big clue.

Another big clue is a negative attitude to the entire concept of parenting; though it's not foolproof, a vehemently negative attitude towards becoming a parent oneself can be a strong indicator of a troubled upbringing. While not wanting children can be a perfectly legitimate life choice, you're listening for the *way* that people justify this choice, and the emotion behind the justification.

Notice a person's ability to self-regulate or parent themselves. If someone is disorganized, chaotic, and generally undisciplined, this may of course point to a permissive upbringing. Be on the lookout for a blatant disregard for rules, disrespect for authority, or a struggle with self-discipline, such as overeating or an alcohol problem.

Pay attention to a person's attitude towards their own needs. If they are self-neglectful, avoidant, or have poor self-worth, they may have had uninvolved or neglectful parents. Such people can often struggle with maintaining stability, be it financial or relational. Observe whether they are consistently in the habit of "going it alone" and fending for themselves. They may have difficulty engaging with people older than them, or have poor social skills in general.

Watch how they parent their own children. This one can be tricky, because it can go one of two ways: a parent may consciously decide to raise their own children differently to the way they were raised (in which case, you can assume that their childhood was the opposite of the one they're trying to offer their children), or they may unconsciously fall into all the same old patterns their parents did. Watch closely for other information to determine which it is.

It's logical to assume that anyone who expressly mentions that they wish to do better than their own parents perceived something lacking in their own upbringing, whereas a person raised in a balanced and healthy way will naturally strive to repeat their parents' choices. People raised with healthy, authoritative parents are often very ready to express gratitude and appreciation for the traditions of the past, and seldom express a desire to rebel against the previous generation.

Once you've got a better idea of a person's family background, you are empowered to relate to that person in a way that they are likely to be most receptive to. Because parenting style affects almost everything else in life (attachment, communication, identity, etc.)

knowing this crucial piece of information lets you recognize the psychological strengths and blind spots of the people you encounter. For example, if they had authoritarian parents, you could make a conscious choice never to communicate in a domineering or inflexible way; likewise, if you know that someone has been raised by neglectful or absent parents, you can cut them some slack when you notice them being a little avoidant or ambivalent.

We don't try to pigeon-hole people just for fun or to flex our armchair-psychologist muscle; rather, we do it to generate real understanding of how other people tick. With practice, this kind of in-depth analysis really is possible within minutes of meeting someone new or based on just a short conversation. The next time you hear someone express glee at offending a "selfish old boomer" or share a fond wish to leave a precious heirloom to their own children, or casually mention how often they used to bunk school, you'll know that these seemingly unimportant remarks may contain fascinating insights about the person speaking. Keep your ears pricked and you may discover that people really can reveal their entire lives in a sentence or two, a gesture, or a smile. This is the joy of becoming a masterful people-reader.

Takeaways:

- We are all products of our environments, and this is especially accurate when we think about the way we were brought up. This is the period of time when our values and worldview are cemented, subconsciously at least. It's where we learn how the world feels about us and how we feel about it in turn. These impressions run deep and affect our daily actions even far into adulthood. The point is not to take a fatalistic view that things cannot change, but rather to use this information to better analyze people.

- The way we feel about relationships and close friendships is highly reflected in what are called attachment styles. These are subconscious assessments of our primary caregivers when we were growing up. However secure, anxious, detached, or safe we were made to feel is something that stays with us. It teaches us how we must regard others, whether accurately or not. There are four styles: secure, anxious-preoccupied, dismissive-avoidant, fearful-avoidant.

- The next way that our upbringing impacts us is through our self-esteem and self-belief. There are an almost infinite number of angles to approach this through, but the general thought is that whatever environments are created for the child persist as a set of beliefs and expectations into adulthood. This heavily involves the judgments and criticisms (or praise) that our caregivers heap onto us. These can have healthy or toxic effects—for our purposes, it's just information to read people and make guesses about their other character traits.

- There is a persisting theory in the world of developmental psychology called the birth order theory. It's not quite anecdotal, but it's also not held as a definitive theory of personality development. It simply states that first borns, second borns, and third borns all have distinct traits that arise out of coping with new and different family dynamics with the caregivers. First borns carry the burden of their parents' expectations, second borns are generally more prone to seeking attention, and third borns are free to roam wherever they please.

- There are four broad parenting styles– authoritarian, permissive, uninvolved, and authoritative. Each leaves its mark on the child as they grow. By observing the way that people talk about their own children or parents, the way that they respond to authority, and the way that they self-regulate, you can get hints about the way their early life has shaped them.

Summary Guide

Chapter 1. People Analysis

- Seeking to analyze people and discover personality and identity has been a compelling issue for as long as we have been sentient beings. To understand ourselves is to make the best decisions, and to understand others provides the ability to make the most out of interactions, whatever your goal. Like many disciplines, study seems to have begun in ancient Greece with the theory of humorism—where four separate bodily fluids were present in the body in varying quantities that gave rise to different personalities and four temperaments in particular.
- One of the most seminal personality theories was put forth by Sigmund Freud hundreds of years later. This is known as the structural model, and you know it by its three components: the id, ego, and superego. Like the humors, they worked together in varying amounts to form a unique personality. The id is a hedonist, the ego is the mediator, while the superego is the conscience.

- There is also a strong biological basis for differences in personality, identity, and the traits we might analyze in others. First, intrasexual and intersexual traits have formed the baseline for our modern personalities in many ways. Second, there are literal biological and physical differences between those who score differently on the Big Five personality traits.
- Why does this all matter? Well, there are far too many reasons we might want to understand the people around us better and more quickly. And if you don't know where you yourself are coming from and where you are right now, how are you supposed to know where you should go next?

CHAPTER 2. TEST YOUR PERSONALITY

- We start our journey into analyzing people like a psychologist by first taking a look at the various personality tests and seeing what we can glean from them. It turns out, quite a bit, although they can't be said to be definitive measures or categories of people. Mostly, they provide different scales and perspectives through which to view people differently.
- The Big Five personality traits are one of the first attempts to classify people based on specific traits rather than as a whole. You can remember the traits easily with the

acronym OCEAN: openness to experience (trying new things), conscientiousness (being cautious and careful), extroversion (drawing energy from others and social situations), agreeableness (warm and sympathetic), and neuroticism (anxious and high-strung).

- Next, the MBTI, though helpful as a guideline, can sometimes suffer from people treating it like a horoscope and reading into their type what they wish to see about themselves. The MBTI functions on four distinct traits and how much of each trait you are or are not. The traits are generally introverted/extroverted (your general attitude toward others), intuitive/feeling (how you perceive information), thinking/feeling (how you process information), and perceiving/judging (how you implement information). Thus, this creates 16 distinct personality types.

- The MBTI does suffer from some shortcomings, including the usage of stereotyping to classify people, and the lack of consistency when people score differently depending on their current moods and circumstances.

- The Keirsey temperaments are a way of organizing the same information gleaned from the MBTI. Here, there are four distinct temperaments, each with two types of roles instead of 16 personality types. The four temperaments are guardian, artisan, idealistic, and rational. Keirsey estimated that up to 80% of the population fell into the first two temperaments.

- Finally, the Enneagram is the final personality test we cover in this chapter. It is composed of nine general types of personalities: reformer, helper, achiever, individualist, investigator, loyalist, enthusiast, challenger, and peacemaker. Each type is composed of a specific set of traits, and in this way, it functions more similarly to Keirsey's temperaments.

CHAPTER 3. OPEN YOUR EYES

- Finally, we get right into the thick of it. How can we read and analyze people just through sight and observation? We cover two primary aspects: facial expressions and body language. It's important to note that though many aspects have been scientifically proven (with physiological origins), we can't say that simple observations are foolproof. It can never be definitive because there are too many external factors to take into account. But we can better understand what typical things to look for and what we can glean from them.
- We use two types of facial expressions: micro- and macroexpressions.

Macroexpressions are larger, slower, and more obvious. They are also routinely faked and consciously created. Microexpressions are the opposite of all of those things: incredibly quick, almost unperceivable, and unconscious. Psychologist Paul Ekman identified a host of microexpressions for each of the six basic emotions and in particular has also identified microexpressions to indicate nervousness, lying, or deception.

- Body language has a much broader range of possible interpretations. Generally, a relaxed body takes up space, while an anxious body contracts and wants to conceal and comfort itself. There are too many specifics to list in a bullet point, but just keep in mind that the only true way to analyze body language is to first know exactly what someone is like when they are normal.

CHAPTER 4. EMOTIONAL CUES

- We've talked about values and rational intentions that people might have. This chapter focuses on emotional cues that we can use to analyze people, and taken together, we are able to better predict and understand both rational and emotional states.
- Better understanding people's emotions

begins with understanding your own. This comes in the form of emotional intelligence, and Daniel Goleman's conception of emotional intelligence consists of self-awareness (what do I feel and why), self-management (how can I express my emotions safely and learn from them), self-motivation (what makes me happy, and how can I achieve that), and social awareness (what are other people feeling and why. The whole process begins with understanding yourself and then realizing that everyone else has the same amount of unconscious and hidden thoughts that dictate their emotions and actions. It is a way of thinking that must be trained and allows you to pull a significant amount of information from a small interaction.

- Likewise, we must learn to understand subtextual cues better. This is related to the social awareness element of emotional intelligence. We must realize that most communication is covert, and yet most of us are only responding to communication that is overt. This means we frequently miss the true meaning of people's words and actions. The easiest way to adopt this particular method of thinking is to ask, *why did they say that, what are they feeling, and what could it mean?*

CHAPTER 5. JUST ASK

- The traits of analyzing others and self-awareness are inseparable. Knowledge in one realm begets knowledge in the other. This chapter focuses on the ways we can gain valuable information from others by simply asking. Notably, these questions are somewhat indirect and also about behaviors and actions, not intentions or thoughts. Thoughts are too easily corrupted or otherwise simply not representative of what you actually feel. When you can learn about behaviors and actions, you can work from concrete information and analyze with a basis in something real.

- Sometimes the best way to discover something about ourselves is to ask seemingly innocent questions, then read between the lines. The way we answer these types of questions can be more honest and indicative than intentionally trying to figure out your personality and identity. This also begins our process of learning how to analyze information we gain from others and dig below the surface and find possible explanations.

- Besides some specific questions that force people to answer about their values in other terms, we can solicit information through a couple of types of stories. After all, the more we hear someone's internal dialogue, the more insight we can gain. The first way to do this is through the seven stories exercise, which implores you to ask about people's seven greatest accomplishments and write the stories involved in those triumphs. What comes out in the story will tell you more about who they are and what they value.

- The second method to discover yourself is through Carl Jung's personality test, which consists of four questions: name a color, name an animal, name a body of water, and think about a white room. The ensuing adjectives people use to describe each of those answers may tell you something specific about their personality that may not be conscious.

CHAPTER 6. THE MOTIVATION FACTOR

- We've talked about analyzing and predicting behavior based on people's emotions and values, but what about motivation? It turns out there are a few prominent and fairly universal models of motivation that can give you a helpful framework to understand people with. When you can pinpoint what people are motivated by, you can see how everything leads back to it either directly or indirectly.
- Any discussion on motivation must begin with the pleasure principle, which generally states that we move toward pleasure and

move away from pain. If you think about it, this is omnipresent in our daily lives in both minuscule and huge ways. As such, this actually makes people more predictable to understand. What is the pleasure people are seeking, and what is the pain they are avoiding? It's always there in some way.

- Next, we move to the pyramid of needs, otherwise known as Abraham Maslow's hierarchy of needs. It states that we are all seeking various types of needs in various points in our lives; when you can observe which level other people are in, you can understand what they are seeking out and motivated by. The levels of the hierarchy are as follows: physiological fulfillment, safety, love and belonging, self-esteem, and self-actualization. Of course, this model, as well as the next one, also functions based on the pleasure principle.

- David McClelland's model of motivation has only three aspects (though they are broader) than Maslow's hierarchy of needs: affiliation (social interaction and belonging), power, and achievement. Similarly, you can deduce what is motivating people by their actions relatively easily.

- Finally, we come to defense of the ego. This is one of our most powerful motivators, but it is mostly unconscious. Simply put, we act to guard our ego from anything that would make us feel psychologically *less*. In doing so, it is so powerful that it allows us to bend reality and lie to ourselves and others—all outside of our conscious awareness. Defense mechanisms are the ways that we avoid responsibility and negative feelings, and they include denial, rationalization, projection, sublimation, regression, displacement, repression, and reaction formation, to name a few. When you know the ego is in play, it often takes front stage over other motivations.

Chapter 7. Remnants of the Past

- We are all products of our environments, and this is especially accurate when we think about the way we were brought up. This is the period of time when our values and worldview are cemented, subconsciously at least. It's where we learn how the world feels about us and how we feel about it in turn. These impressions run deep and affect our daily actions even far into adulthood. The point is not to take a fatalistic view that things cannot change, but rather to use this information to better analyze people.
- The way we feel about relationships and close friendships is highly reflected in what are called attachment styles. These are subconscious assessments of our primary

caregivers when we were growing up. However secure, anxious, detached, or safe we were made to feel is something that stays with us. It teaches us how we must regard others, whether accurately or not. There are four styles: secure, anxious-preoccupied, dismissive-avoidant, fearful-avoidant.

- The next way that our upbringing impacts us is through our self-esteem and self-belief. There are an almost infinite number of angles to approach this through, but the general thought is that whatever environments are created for the child persist as a set of beliefs and expectations into adulthood. This heavily involves the judgments and criticisms (or praise) that our caregivers heap onto us. These can have healthy or toxic effects—for our purposes, it's just information to read people and make guesses about their other character traits.

- There is a persisting theory in the world of developmental psychology called the birth order theory. It's not quite anecdotal, but it's also not held as a definitive theory of personality development. It simply states that first borns, second borns, and third borns all have distinct traits that arise out of coping with new and different family dynamics with the caregivers. First borns carry the burden of their parents' expectations, second borns are generally more prone to seeking attention, and third borns are free to roam wherever they please.

Made in the USA
Columbia, SC
28 March 2025

55831172R10139